Steve Parish
PUBLISHING

Amazing Facts about Australian
Frogs & Toads

Text: Greg Czechura, Queensland Museum
Photographers: Ian Morris and Steve Parish

AMAZING FACTS — AUSTRALIAN FROGS & TOADS

Contents

INTRODUCTION

AUSTRALIA'S amazing frogs	4
THE LIFE CYCLE of frogs	6
FROG ADAPTATIONS — superbly designed	8
SPECIAL PLACES, special frogs	10
WHAT'S IN A NAME? — identifying frogs	12
EARLY AMPHIBIANS — ancient monsters	14

ANURA — HYLIDAE

GREEN TREE-FROGS — firm favourites	16
GREEN TREE-FROGS with orange eyes	18
LAUGHING TREE-FROGS — jewelled disguises	20
GREEN-EYED FROGS — growlers & whistlers	22
CRYPTIC TREE-FROGS — green & brown disguises	24
SMALL TREE-FROGS — heard but not seen	26
SMALL TREE-FROGS — sedgefrogs	27
WATERFALL FROGS — life in the rapids	28
TORRENT TREE-FROGS — going with the flow	29
ROCKET-FROGS — over the top	30
BELL FROGS — shining gems	32
GREENSTRIPE FROG — racing stripes	34
SNAPPING-FROGS — greedy hunters	35
WATERHOLDING-FROGS — drought cheaters	36
COLLARED FROGS — water seekers	37

ANURA — LIMNODYNASTIDAE

TUSKED FROG — getting big-headed	38
FLETCHER'S FROG — killer tadpoles	39
MOUNTAIN FROGS — splendid isolation	40
MARSH-FROGS — hardy croakers	42
BANJO FROGS — marsh musicians	44
BURROWING FROGS — disappearing act	46
SPADEFOOTS & shovelfoots	48

ANURA — MYOBATRACHIDAE

DAY-FROGS & tinkerfrogs	50
MARSUPIAL FROGS — good parents	52
RHEOBATRACHUS — platypus frogs	53
BARRED FROGS — splendid to behold	54
GUNGANS — the little fake toads	56
CRINIAS — same but different	58
CRINIAS — more of the same	60
PARACRINIA & Geocrinias	61
PSEUDOPHRYNE — an Australian icon	62
WESTERN AUSTRALIAN endemics	64

ANURA — RANIDAE

RANIDAE — the true frogs	65

ANURA — MICROHYLIDAE

MICROHYLIDS — narrow-mouthed frogs	66

ANURA — BUFONIDAE

CANE TOAD — ecological catastrophe	68

FROG THREATS

THREATS TO FROGS — an uncertain future	70
FROG DECLINES — a worldwide threat	72

FROG ENTHUSIASTS

FROG WATCHING — a sensory experience	74
FROG PONDS — backyard biodiversity	76

WEB LINKS & FURTHER READING 78
GLOSSARY 79
INDEX 80

Introduction

Australia's amazing frogs

With their large bulging eyes, soft skins and dependence on water, frogs may seem rather fragile creatures. In reality, they are remarkable animals that have survived almost unchanged for millions of years! Frogs are able to live on the land and in the water, but their biggest advantage is that they can adapt to different environmental conditions.

FROGS ARE THE ONLY NATIVE amphibians in Australia today. They can be found almost anywhere near freshwater — in creeks and streams, lagoons, dams, irrigation systems, tanks and, of course, in backyard ponds.

Frogs are most common in the warm, high rainfall areas of the tropics and subtropics, but some species have learned to live in places that are very "unfriendly" to frogs. These include harsh desert landscapes and the freezing temperatures of the Australian Alps.

Australia has about 216 frog species in a multitude of shapes, colours and sizes. Many are so beautiful that they out-dazzle birds and butterflies. Some frogs have truly amazing lifecycles. One little rainforest frog is even a marsupial!

Scientists and naturalists have always been fascinated by frogs and their place in nature. This fascination with frogs extends to thousands of ordinary people who strive to make their backyards frog-friendly by providing ponds for breeding and plants for shelter. In return, frogs can tell us much about the natural world and the health of our environment.

Right: Dainty Green Tree-frog (*Litoria gracilenta*).

Left: Australian rainforests are the home of many spectacular frogs, such as the Green-eyed Frog (*Litoria genimaculata*).

Top left: Alexandria Toadlet (*Uperoleia orientalis*).

Introduction

ABOUT THIS BOOK

This book provides the reader with an expert overview of Australia's amphibians. The Queensland Museum and Steve Parish Publishing have joined forces once again to bring you the most recent and most amazing facts about a group of animals that are currently experiencing a raft of environmental challenges. The outcome is by no means certain for several frog species, and for many others we can only marvel at their resilience in the face of unprecedented change.

Throughout this book you will find photographs taken by a number of leading nature photographers whose patience and persistence has allowed them to get eyeball to eyeball with their subjects. These vivid images not only help illustrate the information on the page, but may also help you identify a species living in your backyard.

The story of our amazing frogs is presented clearly, in several ways. Each page carries small easy-to-read blocks of text. A facts column offers bite-sized snippets of information to be read at a glance. Periodically you will encounter information under the heading "Conservation Watch" at the top of a page: this informs the reader of the status of some of Australia's amphibian species in their struggle to survive.

Above: Tree-frogs like this Roth's Tree-frog (*Litoria rothii*) often have rounded "discs" or "pads" on finger and toe-tips to help them climb.

AS IN ALL AMAZING FACTS BOOKS, you will find each animal referred to by either its common name or its scientific name. Scientific names are usually written in italics and consist of two parts. The first part is the genus name. A genus is a group of closely related organisms with similar characteristics. The second part of the scientific name is the species name — and usually only members of the same species can breed and produce fertile offspring. Take the two frogs at the bottom of the page opposite as an example. One is *Litoria genimaculata* and the other is *Litoria gracilenta*. Both are members of the same genus (*Litoria*) which means they are closely related. However, their second names are different, meaning that they are a separate species and cannot naturally interbreed.

The *Crinia* froglets on page 58 are an exception to this rule, with some species successfully interbreeding.

the FACTS!

AMPHIBIANS ARE ANIMALS that spend part of their lifecycle in water. Frogs and toads are amphibians with no tails (order: Anura). There are two other groups of amphibians — the "tailed" newts and salamanders (order: Urodela), which look like soft-bodied lizards and the bizarre, worm-like caecilians (order: Gymnophiona). Neither are found in Australia.

FROGS ARE EASILY recognised by their distinctive shape. They have a large head and eyes; an indistinct neck; a short body with no tail; two short front legs with four "fingers" on each; and two long hindlegs that end in five "toes".

THE INTERNAL SKELETON of a frog forms a light-weight rigid frame with a large pelvis (hips) designed to help the animal jump easily.

AMPHIBIANS ARE THE ONLY vertebrate animals that can truly live in two worlds — in water and on land. Dahl's Aquatic Frog (*Litoria dahlii*, below) is common on floodplains of the Northern Territory. Research suggests it may be one of the few native animals that is able to eat the eggs and tadpoles of the poisonous Cane Toad (*Rhinella marina*, formerly *Bufo marinus*) without any ill effect.

The life cycle of frogs

Frogs begin their lives in water as larvae or tadpoles that use internal gills to breathe. Later they become land-dwellers, breathing with their lungs. The process whereby the tadpole is eventually transformed into an adult frog is called "metamorphosis" (from the Greek meta, *meaning "change," and* morphe, *meaning "form").*

A TYPICAL FROG BREEDING CYCLE begins with male frogs gathering around ponds, swamps and puddles to sing and attract females. Each frog and toad species has its own unique breeding call. Some are soft and purring, while others are so loud they are painful to hear. Each female is able to recognise the call of males of her own species. Groups of calling males are known as choruses. Once a male has found his mate, he will cling onto her back (amplexus) and fertilise the eggs as she lays them in or near water.

the FACTS!

FROGS, LIKE ALL AMPHIBIANS, are cold-blooded, meaning that their body temperatures change with the temperature of their surroundings. When temperatures fall, some frogs burrow underground, in mud at the bottom of ponds, or hide in any natural nook or cranny. Tadpoles may be protected from some temperature changes because water loses heat more slowly than air.

FROGS WERE PROBABLY THE FIRST animals on Earth to develop vocal cords.

TADPOLES PASS THROUGH 46 different stages from egg to tadpole. The length of time that it takes to complete metamorphosis differs from species to species. The rate of development also depends on temperature and is quicker when it is warmer. A partially metamorphosed Red Tree-frog (*Litoria rubella*), is pictured below.

MALE FROGS CALL for three main reasons: to attract a mate (breeding call), to defend territory or to warn other frogs of danger. Both sexes can make noises, especially when distressed, but only males can make the breeding call.

Above: Male frogs, like the Tyler's Tree-frog (*Litoria tyleri*) inflate their vocal sacs when calling to amplify their sound.

EGGS & TADPOLES

The egg-mass laid by the female frog is known as spawn. Some frogs lay single or small scattered groups of eggs, while others lay their eggs in a clear gel or white foam that floats on the surface of the water. Each fertilised egg hatches into a tadpole, which has a rounded body and a tail with a fin for swimming.

Right: Breeding cycles for frogs are triggered by various factors including the length of the day, rainfall, temperature and humidity. Most frogs breed during spring or summer. Wotjulum Frogs (*Litoria wotjulumensis*) are common across northern Australia.

Above: Many frogs, like the Green Tree-frog (*Litoria caerulea*) breed "explosively" — they congregate in large numbers around water when conditions are right for mating and egg-laying. These frogs lay hundreds, if not thousands, of small eggs (spawn) and provide little or no care for their young. Only a small number of tadpoles will survive to become adult frogs.

METAMORPHOSIS

After hatching, tadpoles attach themselves to weeds or other aquatic plants before they begin to swim, feed and grow.

The metamorphosis of tadpoles into frogs demands massive internal and external changes and is more dramatic than in other amphibians. The process begins with the body becoming longer and the head more distinct. The tadpole grows its hindlimbs and then its forelimbs from tiny "buds" on the sides of its body.

Eventually, the tail is reduced to a stub and disappears. When the changes are complete, the young frog leaves the water looking like a miniature frog.

Most frogs follow a "normal" life cycle and leave their eggs and tadpoles unattended, but some species will build and defend "nests". A small number will lay fewer eggs and care for the tadpoles to increase their chances of survival.

Above left: Two stages in the development of Striped Marsh-frog (*Limnodynastes peronii*) tadpoles.

Left: The tadpole of the Masked Frog (*Litoria personata*) has very distinctive stripes.

the FACTS!

FROGS ALWAYS FERTILISE their eggs as they are laid. This is called external fertilisation.

SOME SALAMANDERS stay as larvae for life. One of the most well known of these larval salamanders is the Axolotl (*Ambystoma mexicanum*) which is often kept as a pet. This amphibian is incorrectly known as the Mexican Walking Fish.

ONE OF THE STRANGEST forms of parental care occurred in Australia's now extinct Platypus or Gastric-brooding Frogs (*Rheobatrachus* spp., below). The tadpoles were raised in the stomach of the female after they had been fertilised and swallowed. The young frogs were "born" when they left the mother's mouth.

MANY TEMPERATE FROG species congregate in large numbers around water for only a night or two each year, when all mating takes place. Tropical species may breed year-round.

TADPOLES COME IN MANY shapes and sizes. The tadpoles of Australian frogs have seventeen basic body types. Each is defined by such features as shape and size of the body, tail and fin as well as colour, type of mouth and behaviour.

Frog adaptations
— superbly designed

Frogs are relatively small animals — giant amphibians became extinct long ago. Modern frogs vary in body length from less than 1 cm to 30 cm, but all of them share the same basic body plan, which can be altered to suit particular lifestyles.

THE ANATOMY (internal structure) of frogs is very similar to other amphibians, but much simpler than that of reptiles, birds and mammals. The frog body is divided into a head, short neck and a trunk (torso). The flat head contains the brain, mouth, eyes, ears and nose. Only limited head movement is possible with the short, almost rigid neck. The stubby trunk forms walls for a single body cavity, called the coelom.

Like other vertebrate animals, a frog's body is supported and protected by a bony skeleton. A frog's teeth grow in the upper jaw and roof of the mouth. They lack roots and are replaced intermittently. Frogs do not chew with these teeth, instead they use their long, flexible, sticky tongue to capture prey and then swallow it whole!

Above: The anatomical modifications for jumping and hopping can easily be seen in a back view. Note the wide "hips" and long hindlegs.

the FACTS!

GROUND-DWELLING FROGS are typically robust with rather claw-like tips to the fingers and toes. Many have warty skin covered with numerous skin glands.

FROGS THAT LIVE ALONG STREAMS often have small discs on the tips of their fingers to help them move over wet, slippery surfaces. Most tend to be coloured to blend with the background.

CLIMBING FROGS have large discs on the tips of their broad fingers and toes, to help them grip leaves and branches. Some are able to cling to smooth vertical surfaces like glass or mossy rocks. Tree-frogs often have smooth skin.

LIVING CATAPULT

A frog does not have any ribs and has only nine vertebrae in its backbone. The vertebrae at the end of the backbone are fused together to form a long rod-like bone called the "urostyle". This is the only indication that the ancestors of frogs once grew tails. The urostyle transfers power from the frog's legs to its body during jumping or swimming, while the long pelvis has a moveable joint that allows it to slide up and down the backbone. This helps catapult the frog into the air. The "arms" and "legs" of the frog are made up of a single bone in the upper and lower sections and end in four "fingers" and five "toes". Frogs' hindlegs are much longer than their forelimbs and are designed for swimming and leaping. All species of frogs can swim.

FROGS BREATHE with their lungs and also through their skin. An extensive network of blood vessels allows oxygen in the air to pass through the skin and directly enter the bloodstream. A submerged frog will only breathe through its skin, obtaining all of its oxygen from the water.

A SPECIAL SKIN

Frogs must keep their skin in good order by staying clean and moist. Mucous glands lubricate the skin and protect the frog from drying out. Some of the bumps and warts on frog skin are glands that produce poisons and protective chemicals to deter bacteria, fungi and other micro-organisms. Frogs are able to shed the outer layer of skin by twisting and stretching. They often eat the dead skin as it comes off. This is called keratophagy.

COAT OF MANY COLOURS

Frogs can be almost any colour of the rainbow. Some are clad in camouflage colours and have rough-textured skin to blend with their surroundings. Others have bright colours on the backs of their legs, groin and "armpits" to dazzle or distract predators. The colour of frog skin is produced by layers of pigmented cells and most frogs can change the brightness of their skin by moving dark pigment along special cells called melanophores.

SEE NO EVIL

The sense organs of frogs vary greatly. Some have acute vision, but some frogs that live underground have tiny, almost useless eyes. Frogs have simple eyes with fixed lenses that cannot change focus. To close its eyes, a frog simply draws the eyes into their sockets. Frogs have a good sense of smell, but hearing varies. Frogs do not have external ears and their circular eardrums (tympanic membranes) are exposed.

Left, top to bottom: Kunapalari Frog (*Neobatrachus kunapalari*); Dainty Green Tree-frog (*Litoria gracilenta*); Desert Spadefoot Frog (*Notaden nichollsi*).

the FACTS!

THE FACT THAT FROGS can absorb oxygen and water through their skin makes them particularly vulnerable to pollutants in the air or water. Even when they don't ingest these substances through their mouths, they can still suffer the effects. This sensitivity also makes frogs excellent biological indicators for scientists studying the health of the environment.

FROGS MAINLY EAT INSECTS and other invertebrates but they will eat any animal that they can catch and overpower. This Marbled Marsh-frog (*Limnodynastes convexiusculus*, below) is attempting to make a meal of a Roth's Tree-frog (*Litoria rothii*).

MANY AUSTRALIAN FROGS have toxic skin secretions. Some of these can cause irritation on contact with the eyes but no native frogs are considered to be dangerous. The introduced Cane Toad is able to produce large quantities of poison from its skin glands and is a threat to wildlife, pets and people.

Special places, special frogs

Australian frogs can be found across the continent from the high country of the Australian Alps to the harsh deserts of the Outback. Some frogs are habitat generalists that can live almost anywhere but there are other species, habitat specialists, that can only survive in very specific conditions.

THE EARLIEST AUSTRALIAN FROGS inhabited dense rainforests that covered most of the continent about 10–12 million years ago. Since then, the climate has become much drier and rainforests are now only found in northern and eastern Australia. As the rainforests dwindled, so did the number of frog species found there. Living rainforest species are almost all habitat specialists and include some of the most amazing Australian frogs such as the Pouched Frog (*Assa darlingtoni*).

the FACTS!

FROGS THAT LIVE NEAR NOISY, fast-flowing streams can't always hear mating calls above the roar of water. Instead, they signal their intentions by "waving" to prospective partners.

THE TADPOLES of some rainforest frogs take over a year to change into frogs.

SOME TYPES OF COLOUR variation in frogs are due to genetic mutation; one sometimes seen in green frogs is a blue mutation (above).

AUSTRALIA'S TROPICAL RAINFORESTS are home to around one quarter of all Australian frog species.

THE WALLUM SEDGEFROG (*Litoria olongburensis*, below) lives in wallum heath and can often be found sheltering in waterside grasses and sedges.

Above: Australian frogs come in many shapes, forms and colours. Many small species, toadlets and froglets are drab coloured, but others sport brightly coloured patches on their head, body or limbs, like this aptly named Red-crowned Toadlet (*Pseudophryne australis*).

CLIMB EVERY MOUNTAIN

As climates change, mountains often act as refuge for animals that need cool, mild conditions to survive. Habitats that are lost elsewhere can be preserved on mountains, which also have their own special habitats, such as boulder and snow fields. The Black Mountain Boulderfrog (*Cophixalus saxatilis*) only lives among boulders on a particular mountain near Cooktown, in north Queensland. The mountain frogs (*Philoria* spp.) and the torrent and tinker frogs (*Taudactylus* spp.) are only found in high altitude rainforests.

Right: Fleay's Barred Frog (*Mixophyes fleayi*) lives in montane rainforest. It is named in honour of the late naturalist David Fleay.

Introduction

UP THE CREEK

Some frogs are able to live in flowing water, even where the current is strong or the water cascades. Stream frogs "glue" their eggs to immoveable objects like rocks to stop them being washed away. They also lay larger eggs and their tadpoles are more developed. Others spawn in less turbulent parts of the watercourse.

Left: Stream-dwelling frogs are strong swimmers. They include barred frogs (*Mixophyes* spp.), tree-frogs and rocket-frogs (*Litoria* spp.), such as the Stony-creek Frog (*Litoria wilcoxii,* pictured).

the FACTS!

BURROWING FROGS use special hardened structures, known as tubercles, on the palms of their hands and/or soles of their feet to assist with digging.

FROGS DIG into the ground either head first, or backwards like this Ornate Burrowing Frog (*Opisthodon ornatus*, below).

SOME BURROWING FROGS descend in a corkscrew fashion. They use their hindfeet to shovel soil aside and rotate as they do so.

ACID FROGS

Heathlands are exposed areas that have small, stunted shrubs and very few trees. Soils are very poor and can be boggy, peaty, sandy or stony. Only very special frogs can survive these conditions, which include highly acidic waters. Frogs that live in these areas are often called "acid frogs" and they include several species of tree-frogs (*Litoria* spp.) and the Wallum Froglet (*Crinia tinnula*).

Right: The Freycinet's Frog (*Litoria freycineti*) occurs in coastal wallum heaths of southern Queensland and Northern New South Wales.

WATER RESTRICTIONS

Deserts are extreme environments where water is scarce. Normally, this would make life impossible for frogs, but some burrow down into the soil to escape heat and conserve moisture. Some even form cocoons using layers of their old outer skin and mucus. The water-holding frogs (*Cyclorana* spp.), store large amounts of water in their bladder. Desert frogs only appear after rain and quickly disappear when the waters recede.

Left: Desert frogs, like this Desert Spadefoot Frog (*Notaden nichollsi)*, are burrowers that only "appear" after rains and floods.

Introduction

What's in a name?
— identifying frogs

Naming and identifying things is fundamental to how humans make sense of the world around them. Amphibians come in many shapes and forms — a frog is different to a salamander and there are different types of frogs. The process of naming and identifying plants and animals is called classification.

SCIENTISTS AROUND THE WORLD use a recognised system of classification for naming and describing plants and animals. The "Linnaean system" was developed by eighteenth century Swedish botanist, Carolus Linnaeus, and it gives each plant or animal its own place in the natural order of things. Living organisms are first divided into broad categories, such as animal or plant, and then into smaller groups down to the level of an individual type of animal. As part of this process, each living thing is given a scientific name. This Latin-based name is recognised by scientists everywhere and identifies an animal's relationship to others of its type.

the FACTS!

THERE ARE MORE THAN 6240 KNOWN SPECIES of frogs, salamanders and caecilians belonging to 475 genera and 56 families. Of these, 5503 species are frogs and toads, 564 are newts and salamanders and 173 are caecilians. The number of species grows each year as new animals are discovered. Since 1985 the total number of recognised amphibian species has increased by nearly 35%.

CONTRARY TO POPULAR OPINION, not all frogs are green with smooth skins and not all toads are brown with warty skins. The names "frog" and "toad" do not have any real scientific meaning simply because they are used to describe many unrelated species of amphibian (anurans) with no tail.

THE SCIENCE OF CLASSIFYING (describing and naming) plants and animals is called taxonomy.

MICHAEL CERMAK

Above: The Waterfall Frog or Torrent Tree-frog (*Litoria nannotis*) is one of a number of tree-frogs (family: Hylidae) that live in fast flowing mountain streams and torrents. Although these frogs have similar habits and belong to the same frog family, they may not be closely related to each other. The closest relatives of the Waterfall Frog are several species known as mistfrogs that live in the Wet Tropics of north-east Queensland.

CLASSIFYING THE WATERFALL FROG

CATEGORY	NAME	ANIMALS
Kingdom	Animalia	All animals
Phylum	Chordata	Animals with a nerve chord along back
Subphylum	Vertebrata	Chordates with jointed bony backbones
Class	Amphibia	Vertebrates that lay their eggs and live in the water during the early part of their life cycle before moving to the land as adults
Order	Anura	Short-bodied, tailless amphibians
Family	Hylidae	Tree-frogs and relatives
Subfamily	Pelodryadinae	Australian tree-frogs, rocket-frogs, mistfrogs, bell frogs, lace-lids, collared-frogs and water-holding frogs
Genus	*Litoria*	Australian tree-frogs
Species	*nannotis*	Waterfall Frog (or Torrent Tree-frog)

FAMILY GROUPS

Australia is home to nearly 220 native and one introduced species of frogs and toads that belong to six different families. They range in size from tiny 1.4–2 cm tree-frogs, froglets and toadlets to White-lipped Tree-frogs (*Litoria infrafrenata*) and Giant Barred Frogs (*Mixophyes iteratus*) that grow to 11–11.5 cm in length.

FAMILY: HYLIDAE
Tree-frogs

This family contains many of the world's 830 species of tree-frog. Australian tree-frogs belong to a distinct sub-family — the Pelodryadinae. These "tree-frogs" also includes some ground-dwellers and even a few species that burrow.

Above: Green Tree-frog (*Litoria caerulea*).

FAMILY: MYOBATRACHIDAE
Australian water frogs

This group of 87 species includes all of Australia's froglets and toadlets. Three species are found in New Guinea. These animals are also known as the Australian parental-care frogs because some species care for their eggs and young.

Above: Floodplain Toadlet (*Uperoleia inundata*).

FAMILY: LIMNODYNASTIDAE
Australian ground frogs

Marsh and burrowing frogs make up this family group, which includes 40 species of Australian ground frogs. Of these, four species are found only in New Guinea.

Above: Scarlet-sided Pobblebonk (*Limnodynastes terraereginae*).

FAMILY: MICROHYLIDAE
Narrow-mouthed frogs

There are 419 species of narrow-mouthed frogs worldwide and, of these, 215 occur in Australasia. Most live in New Guinea, but some also inhabit the rainforests and vine scrubs of tropical northern Australia.

Above: Ornate Nursery-frog (*Cophixalus ornatus*).

FAMILY: RANIDAE
"True" frogs

Only a single species of this widespread family of frogs occurs in coastal areas of Queensland and the Northern Territory, although several others are found in New Guinea and the surrounding islands.

Above: Australian Wood Frog (*Sylvirana daemeli*).

FAMILY: BUFONIDAE
"True" toads

The introduced Cane Toad (*Rhinella marina*, formerly *Bufo marinus*) is the only member of this group in Australia and New Guinea, where it is an invasive pest. "True" toads are a large and diverse group with 495 species worldwide, particularly in South-East Asia and the islands to Australia's north.

Above: Cane Toad (*Rhinella marina*).

Early amphibians
— ancient monsters

The first amphibians were the labyrinthodonts, which lived more than 300 million years ago. They looked similar to the giant newts or salamanders that exist today because they had long bodies, short limbs, broad flat heads and finned tails.

THEIR MOUTHS WERE ALSO FILLED with rows of sharp teeth, ideal for catching fish, insects and other amphibians! The animals were given their common name because of the way the internal layers of the teeth are folded to resemble a labyrinth or maze. The largest labyrinthodonts grew about 4–5 m long, but smaller species were about 1 m.

There were many various kinds of prehistoric amphibians during the late Palaeozoic Era (354–250 million years ago). Most early amphibians became extinct around 250 million years ago during a Mass Extinction at the end of the Permian Period. Just as Australia later became a haven for marsupials, it played a similar role for labyrinthodonts, which survived here until the Cretaceous Period 141–65 million years ago.

the FACTS!

NEWTS AND SALAMANDERS (tailed amphibians), like the giant salamanders (*Andrius* spp., above) and the Axolotl (*Ambystoma mexicanum*, below) resemble early amphibians in appearance. Tailed amphibians do not occur in the Australasian region.

FOSSILS OF FROGS and salamanders show that these animals have existed since at least the Jurassic Period. Caecilian fossils are rare, but short-legged amphibians that otherwise resembled caecilians also existed during the Jurassic. The rarity of caecilian fossils is probably due to their burrowing habitat and reduced skeleton, both of which lessen the chances of preservation.

THE EARLIEST AMPHIBIAN was an animal known as *Elginerpeton pancheni*, which lived in Scotland around 368 million years ago.

THE EARLIEST FROG-LIKE AMPHIBIAN is *Triadobatrachus massinoti*. Fossils of this 250-million-year-old animal have been found in Madagascar. Its skull is frog-like and has large eye-sockets but the rest of the skeleton is unlike a frog. Its long body, short tail and other differences in the skeleton suggest that *Triadobatrachus* could not jump like a frog.

Above: The one metre long labyrinthodont *Parotosuchus gungunj* lived during the Triassic. Its fossils have been found at Rewan, Central Queensland.

LAST SURVIVORS

Australian labyrinthodonts included *Siderops kehli* and *Koolasuchus cleelandi*. Fossils of *Siderops* have been found in southern Queensland. It lived during the Jurassic Period 205–141 million years ago. *Siderops* was about 2.5 m long and had a huge, tooth-filled mouth. *Koolsuchus* was the last Australian labyrinthodont and may have been the very last in the world. It did not become extinct until about 120 million years ago.

Right: Siderops kelhi grew up to 3 m. It may have been a waterside ambush predator.

THE OLDEST FROGS

Frog fossils have been found on all continents, including Antarctica. The oldest is *Prosalirus bitis*, which lived in North America 180–185 million years ago. Other early frogs include *Vieraella* and *Notobatrachus* (family: Leiopelmatidae) and *Eodiscoglossus* (family: Discoglossidae), which lived alongside the dinosaurs during the Jurassic Period. Some primitive frogs from these or related families still survive in New Zealand, along the west coast of North America, in Europe and in parts of Asia and South America. The oldest fossils of modern frogs show that these animals date back to around 125 million years ago and that they also lived with dinosaurs.

Above: The Australian labyrinthodont, *Koolasuchus cleelandi*, may have been the very last of its kind. It became extinct during the Cretaceous Period.

FOSSILS DOWN UNDER

Australia's oldest frog fossils (10–30 million-years-old) come from Lake Palankarinna in South Australia. They include *Australobatrachus ilius*, two species of tree-frog (*Litoria* spp.) and a marsh-frog (*Limnodynastes archeri*). Frog fossils have also been found at a number of other sites, including: Lake Yanda South Australia; Riversleigh and Mt Etna in Queensland; King Island in Bass Strait; and at several sites in Western Australia, including Devil's Lair at Margaret River.

Right, top to bottom: Some frog fossils are indistinguishable from current living species — Fletcher's Frog (*Lechriodus fletcheri*); Striped Marsh-frog (*Limnodynastes peronii*).

the FACTS!

XENOBRACHYOPS ALLOS (above) was one of a number of broad-headed Triassic amphibians. It grew to 50 cm and fed on insects and fish.

ABOUT 75% of all amphibian families and about 80% of reptiles became extinct at the end of the Permian Period, about 250 million years ago. The extinction was due to a worldwide climatic change that lowered temperatures and created more seasonal climates.

IN THE PAST, there were many more types of amphibians, but they do not have any living representatives. Fossil species are classified and named using the Linnaean system.

AUSTRALIAN LABYRINTHODONT *Koolasuchus* is known mainly from jaw fragments found in Victoria. These suggest the animal grew to 4–5 m long.

THE REMAINS of at least 20 frog species have been found at the Riversleigh fossil site in north-west Queensland; this may be the richest deposit of frog fossils in the world.

Green tree-frogs
— firm favourites

Order: Anura
Family: Hylidae

Climbing frogs like the tree-frogs are easy to recognise. They have flattened discs on the tips of their fingers and toes. These discs allow them to "stick" to smooth objects and detach when they need to move.

FROGS' TOE PADS are coated with thin mucous, which sticks to surfaces in much the same way that wet tissue paper sticks to glass. On sloping surfaces such as tree trunks and leaves, climbing frogs must continually adjust the angle of their toes to maintain the best grip and distribution of weight. The process by which they detach their toe pads is called peeling. It is similar to someone removing sticking plaster and this can be done very quickly if the frog needs to escape predators.

the FACTS!

GREEN TREE-FROGS breed mainly in spring and summer after rain. Breeding choruses are noisy affairs because hundreds, if not thousands, of males gather quickly around temporary pools, puddles and swamps to attract mates. They will even breed in water troughs and buckets that have filled with rainwater.

GREEN TREE-FROG TADPOLES take around 31–40 days to metamorphose provided that temperatures stay around 30°C.

THE GREEN TREE-FROG is not only popular with Australians. It has long been widely sold as a pet, under the name "White's Tree-frog", in the USA and Europe.

IN AUSTRALIA, it is really not necessary to make a pet of a Green Tree-frog because they frequently take up residence in gutter pipes, pot plants, mailboxes, bathrooms, laundries and other spaces. It is common to hear stories of Green Tree-frogs being moved, only to return a few days later.

Above: Green Tree-frogs are smooth skinned and usually bright green, becoming more olive-brown to grey when inactive. Some have white spots on their back, sides and legs. The backs of the thighs are yellow to maroon. They are often found in gardens and around buildings.

THE SMILING CROAKER

The Green Tree-frog (*Litoria caerulea*) is probably Australia's most popular and best known frog. Much of its popularity is due to its placid nature and "smiling" face.

This large attractive frog is found across northern Australia, most of Queensland and eastern New South Wales.

Very few Australian frogs make a croaking call — most whistle, cackle, grunt, moan and chime — but the Green Tree-frog is one of the few that do croak. Green Tree-frogs grow up to around 11 cm in body length and, like most frogs, the females are much larger than males.

Above: Adult Green Tree-frogs have large glands on the back of the head, which look like rolls of thick skin. They will eat small birds and mammals, such as mice and bats.

Anura — Hylidae

Conservation Watch
All of the large green tree-frogs are considered to be Secure.

MAGNIFICENT TREE-FROG

Bright colouring makes the Magnificent Tree-frog (*Litoria splendida*) one of Australia's most spectacular frogs. Its back is bright green to olive with scattered yellow or white spots and blotches. Its belly is white and the inner parts of its legs and groin are bright orange-yellow. This frog grows to 10 cm and lives in caves, rock crevices and is often found around buildings, shower blocks, water tanks and toilets in the Kimberley region of Western Australia.

Above and right: The Magnificent Tree-frog has a huge gland covering the top of its head. It is very closely related to the Green Tree-frog.

GIANT AMONGST FROGS

The White-lipped Tree-frog (*Litoria infrafrenata*) grows to 13.5 cm and is Australia's largest frog; it may also be the largest tree-frog in the world. It has a bright green to olive back and its belly is white. A conspicuous white stripe lines the lower jaw. The White-lipped Tree-frog is found on Cape York Peninsula and in the Wet Tropics of north-east Queensland, New Guinea and parts of Indonesia. It has a loud, harsh call resembling the barking of a dog. Like the Green Tree-frog, it feeds mainly on insects, but will eat mice, bats and small birds if the opportunity arises.

Right: The White-lipped Tree-frog has large pads on its fingers and toes. It is also known as the Giant Tree-frog.

the FACTS!

THE CAVE-DWELLING FROG (*Litoria cavernicola*) from the Kimberley region of Western Australia grows to 5.5 cm. As its common name suggests, this frog lives in caves and between boulders on rock plateaus. It is dull green to greenish-brown with a whitish belly.

GREEN TREE-FROGS often announce the approach of rain by loud croaking in downpipes and letterboxes.

THE LARGE GLAND on the Magnificent Tree-frog's head becomes larger as the frog ages.

JOURNEY TO THE CENTRE

Rock gorges with waterholes in Central Australia are the favoured habitat of the Centralian Tree-frog (*Litoria gilleni*), which is often found hiding beneath boulders during the day. Centralian Tree-frogs have a dark olive to bright green back, with small creamy-white spots and blotches. There is often a white streak, or a number of white spots that run from the corner of the mouth to the base of the arm.

Left: Large specimens of the Centralian Tree-frog reach around 7 cm in body length.

GREEN TREE-FROGS mainly eat insects but they will also eat small birds, mice and bats. It is not uncommon to find them lurking around microbat roosts and snatching small bats that pass by.

Green tree-frogs with orange eyes

Order: Anura
Family: Hylidae

Green and gold are Australia's sporting colours and they are also the colours of three pretty tree-frogs that live along the coastal parts of eastern Australia. Two are found in or near rainforest and wet eucalypt forest, while the third favours lush vegetation of almost any description — including parks and gardens.

THE DAINTY GREEN (or Graceful) Tree-frog (*Litoria gracilenta*) lives in a variety of habitats, but predominantly in coastal woodlands and forests from Cape York to Northern New South Wales. It is easiest to find in dense vegetation near marshes, lagoons, drains and flooded areas after rain and especially in the warmer months.

The frogs commonly hide in foliage, or rest on leaves, with their eyes closed and legs tucked tightly into their bodies. They are bright leaf-green to lime-green with a contrasting bright yellow belly and orange eyes. A faint yellow-green stripe runs from the nostril over the eye. The upper arms, thighs, fingers and toes are yellow and the backs of the thighs are purplish-brown with an iridescent blue sheen.

Above: Male Dainty Green Tree-frogs call from the ground, hidden among grass and foliage, or perched on plants that overhang water.

the FACTS!

DAINTY GREEN TREE-FROGS are more common in lowland areas than in mountains or highlands.

DAINTY GREEN TREE-FROGS rest in the foliage of trees and shrubs and are often found by gardeners while pruning shrubs or lopping trees. It is a good idea to check foliage destined for mulchers to prevent the frogs being mulched.

WARM, WET, HUMID SUMMER nights are when Dainty Green Tree-frogs are most active. Males call from above ground before they form breeding choruses at suitable ponds or marshes.

AT THE APPROACH OF DANGER many frogs will jump away, others like the Dainty Green Tree-frog crouch and remain still. They attempt to avoid detection by not drawing attention to themselves.

SUMMER LOVIN'

Male Dainty Green Tree-frogs call at night, typically after spring and summer rains, and form large choruses around shallow water. They call from the ground or perched on plants that overhang water. The breeding call is a long, moaning "aaaare".

The frogs take advantage of almost any temporary water and will lay eggs in buckets and other water containers, as well as swimming pools. Eggs are laid in a single layer of clear jelly just below the water surface, or in clusters attached to floating vegetation.

Tadpoles are about 4.5 cm long and have a dark brown, oval-shaped body, which has a gold tinge in bright light.

Above: Dainty Green Tree-frogs make the most of summer rains to breed.

Conservation Watch
Dainty Green Tree-frogs, Orange-eyed Tree-frogs and Orange-thighed Tree-frogs are all considered to be Secure.

ORANGE-EYED TREE-FROG

The Orange-eyed Tree-frog (*Litoria chloris*) is the largest of the red and orange-eyed tree-frogs, growing up to 6.5 cm in body length. Its striking eyes are orange-red, but become golden near the pupil.

A rainforest inhabitant, this frog also lives in wet eucalypt forests and nearby areas from the central coast of Queensland to Northern New South Wales.

Right: The breeding call of the Orange-eyed Tree-frog is a series of rising "aarc" sounds followed by a trill.

BANANA BOX FROGS

The Dainty Green Tree-frog (left) is one of a number of tree-frogs that are popularly known as "banana-box frogs" because they are sometimes accidentally transported in fruit from tropical areas to shops and homes in southern Australia. The frogs are also found in vegetables, flowers and nursery plants. Scientists believe it is possible that "banana-box frogs" may spread amphibian diseases from one area to another.

the FACTS!

IT IS POSSIBLE TO FIND individual Dainty Green Tree-frogs that are all yellow. This is an uncommon colour mutation.

IF YOU FIND A "BANANA-BOX FROG" do not release it into the wild. Although the frogs seldom adjust to living outside their native habitat, they may be disease carriers. Contact your local museum or Parks and Wildlife Service for assistance.

LITTLE IS KNOWN about many aspects of the biology of both the Orange-eyed and Orange-thighed Tree-frogs. Both species seem to disappear outside of the breeding season and it is suspected that they hide in the forest canopy during the non-breeding season.

ORANGE-EYED and Orange-thighed Tree-frogs will breed in almost any suitable puddle of water, including the flooded wheel-ruts and drains along bush tracks. Some males call from overhanging branches while others call from the ground or along the water's edge.

ORANGE-EYED TREE-FROGS call from rainwater tanks and may occasionally attempt to breed there.

BREEDING CHORUSES of Orange-eyed and Orange-thighed Tree-frogs frequently extend along slow-flowing streams or backwaters.

ORANGE-THIGHED TREE-FROG

The Orange-thighed Tree-frog (*Litoria xanthomera*) lives in the rainforests of Tropical North Queensland. It is poorly known but otherwise seems similar to the Orange-eyed Tree-frog. During spring and summer, males call from along streams and around ponds and waterholes. The breeding call is a long moaning "waaarc", then softer trills.

Left: Bright orange flashes on the back of the thighs give the frog its common name. The Orange-thighed Tree-frog grows to 5.5 cm long and is bright green with a white, lemon-yellow or orange belly.

Laughing tree-frogs
— jewelled disguises

Order: Anura
Family: Hylidae

It is commonly believed that all frogs are green and all toads are brown, but this isn't so. Some of Australia's most attractive tree-frogs are clad in shades of brown and grey. Different species of brown tree-frogs are just as widespread as their bright green cousins.

the FACTS!

MANY TREE-FROGS are green because they hide in foliage, but not all parts of a tree are green. Brown tree-frogs try to escape detection by blending with tree trunks, branches and even rocks. Some rainforest tree-frogs even have a mossy look to help them blend into their wet surroundings.

ALSO KNOWN AS the Emerald-spotted Tree-frog, the Peron's Tree-frog lives in a range of habitats from forest to open cleared land.

THE PERON'S TREE-FROG (below) has a creamy or yellow belly and its groin, armpits, feet and backs of thighs are mottled with black and yellow.

TADPOLES of Peron's Tree-frogs are fairly large with three long dark stripes down the back and a shiny pale green spot on the tip of the snout. They often swim with their heads facing upwards, which highlights the spot. As they develop, the tadpoles become more olive-brown or yellow-brown.

Above: Peron's Tree-frogs have coarse skin with low warts and lumpy growths and small emerald-green speckles on their backs. Their eyes have cross-shaped marking; they grow to about 5 cm.

A FROG THAT CHANGES ITS SPOTS

Being able to change colour when you need to is a handy talent for an animal. Depending on the time of day, the temperature and its behaviour, Peron's Tree-frog (*Litoria peronii*) is able to do just that. At rest, the frog is pale to creamy with dark flecks, but when active and alert it returns to varying intensities of its usual dark brown or grey. The small emerald-green spots on its back can also fade or become very bright.

Peron's Tree-frogs are often found near rivers, creeks, lagoons and flooded areas as well as in vegetation at some distance from water.

Right: Summer choruses of Peron's Tree-frogs sound like massed cackling or a "concert" of machine-guns or jackhammers.

Conservation Watch
Roth's, Peron's and Tyler's Tree-frogs are all Secure.

ROTH'S TREE-FROG

Roth's Tree-frog (*Litoria rothii*), also known as the Northern Laughing Tree-frog, occurs from the Kimberley region of Western Australia across northern Australia and along the east coast of Queensland. One of the distinctive features of this frog (top left) is its bicoloured iris: the upper half is bright red and the lower half is silvery.

These frogs are good climbers that live high in trees and other tall plants. They are found close to permanent and temporary water — paperbark swamps are a favoured habitat — and their diet consists mainly of adult aquatic insects such as flies and damselflies. During the day they often form tight clusters when they shelter under bark.

Above: The Roth's Tree-frog is the only member of this group of tree-frogs that will be found in northern Australia. It also occurs with the Peron's Tree-frog in parts of coastal southern Queensland.

TYLER'S TREE-FROG

Tyler's (or Southern Laughing) Tree-frogs (*Litoria tyleri*) resemble their northern cousins, but they have a uniformly coloured iris. They are found along the south-east coast of mainland Australia. These tree-frogs live in wet and dry eucalypt forests, coastal swamps and heaths and grasslands. They also frequent gardens and buildings. On warm, wet summer nights, Tyler's Tree-frogs will gather at well-lit windows to feed on insects attracted to the light. They breed throughout spring and summer.

Above: Male Tyler's Tree-frogs call while sitting on low branches, clinging to the trunks of trees, or from near the top of clumps of sedges.

the FACTS!

PERON'S, ROTH'S AND TYLER'S Tree-frogs are very closely related and may be regarded as "sibling species".

IN SOME AREAS, it is possible to find Roth's Tree-frog and one of the laughing tree-frog species breeding at the same pond. This provides a good chance to detect differences in the way each species calls.

ROTH'S TREE-FROG (below) and its relatives (Peron's and Tyler's Tree-frogs) can be found around buildings and other structures. They will breed in garden ponds that are surrounded by plants and rich in insect life.

THE LARGE DISCS on the tips of the fingers and toes, as well as the black and yellow markings in the thighs and groin, distinguish these tree-frogs from Cane Toads.

PERON'S TREE-FROGS are one of a number of frogs that can seem to disappear from an area for many seasons, only to make a dramatic reappearance at some later time.

Green-eyed frogs
— growlers & whistlers

Order: Anura
Family: Hylidae

Tree trunks and rocks in rainforest provide excellent cover for small animals like frogs. Many rainforest frogs have rough or warty skins and colours that help them blend with bark and moss.

THREE SPECIES THAT TAKE ADVANTAGE OF CAMOUFLAGE colouring are the Green-eyed Frog (*Litoria genimaculata*), the Growling Green-eyed Frog (*Litoria eucnemis*) and the Kuranda Tree-frog (*Litoria myola*). All inhabit rainforest and are so similar that scientists once thought they were the same species.

The Green-eyed Frog has been known by many names including the Tapping Green-eyed Frog, New Guinea Tree-frog, Fringe-limbed Tree-frog and Green-eyed Tree-frog. It is usually greyish-brown, silvery or reddish-brown with dark brown mottling and a dark patch between the eyes. Pale patches resembling lichen or moss may be scattered over the back and sides. The rear edge of its front and back legs have a series of small bumps that form a "fringe" to help the frog blend with the surface it is sitting on.

Above: Green-eyed Frogs grow to about 8.5 cm. They are often found along slow flowing creeks and their mating call is a series of soft clicks.

the FACTS!

GREEN-EYED AND Growling Green-eyed Frogs get their common names partly from the small green patch that is always present on the skin at the upper rear of each eye.

GREEN-EYED AND Growling Green-eyed Frogs are also found in New Guinea along with four other very similar species. Two of the related species — *Litoria lutea* and *Litoria thesaurensis* — have green bones that are visible through the belly skin.

THE EGGS of Green-eyed Frogs are laid in firm masses that may contain over 800 eggs. The tadpoles are dark brown.

GREEN-EYED FROG females that are ready to breed may weigh nearly five times as much as males (females 23 g and males 5 g).

KURANDA TREE-FROGS can be best identified by their distinctive short, fast tapping call.

THE BROWN TREE-FROG is found throughout Tasmania, Victoria, parts of South Australia and New South Wales in a range of habitats including coastal lagoons and swamps, wet and dry eucalypt forests, grasslands and bogs.

RUMBLE IN THE JUNGLE

The Growling Green-eyed Frog has several other common names, including the Growling Tree-frog and Fringed Tree-frog. It is very similar in size and appearance to the Green-eyed Frog, but has a different distribution. The Green-eyed Frog inhabits a relatively small area of rainforest along the east coast of Queensland. The Growling Green-eyed Frog is at home in the rainforests of northern Cape York Peninsula, where it is often found near rocky creeks. Like many other amphibians, this frog breeds during spring and summer. Its mating call is a series of short growls, hence its common name.

Right: Skin secretions from Green-eyed and Growling Green-eyed Frogs (pictured) have strong antibiotic properties.

Conservation Watch

The Littlejohn's Tree-frog is regarded as Vulnerable. Threats include a fungal disease, habitat loss and climate change. All others are Secure.

KEEPING IT IN THE FAMILY

Sometimes closely related frogs look so similar and are so much alike in their behaviour that they can only be separated by scientific examination — or geographically, according to where they live. But when two or more similar frogs live in the same habitat it can be a problem not only for the humans trying to identify them, but for individual frogs trying to find a mate.

The Brown Tree-frog (*Litoria ewingii*) and its relatives are one of the most confusing groups of Australian frogs to identify. The related species include the Victorian Frog (*Litoria paraewingi*), Verreaux's Tree-frog (*Litoria verreauxii*), Revealed Frog (*Litoria revelata*), Littlejohn's Tree-frog (*Litoria littlejohni*) and Jervis Bay Tree-frog (*Litoria jervisiensis*). This group of tree-frogs can be found throughout eastern and southern Australia from the Atherton Tableland in north Queensland to Victoria and Tasmania.

All of these frogs are fawn, brown, red-brown or greyish-brown and most have dark flecks and a dark broad band along their back. They all have yellow, red or orange on the backs of their thighs and groin and small discs on the tips of their fingers and toes; a few are different sizes. For example, at 5.5–6 cm, the Jervis Bay and Littlejohn's Tree-frogs are larger than the rest of the group (3–4.5 cm), but size isn't always the answer.

Left: The Brown Tree-frog (pictured), Victorian Frog and Revealed Frog will breed throughout the year after rain, but mainly in early spring and autumn.

DIFFERENT CROAKS FOR DIFFERENT FOLKS

Like the frogs themselves, scientists have learned to listen carefully to the mating calls of the frogs as a way to tell them apart. Each frog species has its own unique breeding call.

The Brown Tree-frog call sounds like a rapid "weep..eep..eep..eep" repeated about 5–15 times. The Victorian Frog makes a "weeeep weeep weep" sound repeated three to seven times. The call of a Verreaux's Tree-frog sounds like "weep...weep...weep", while the Revealed Frog has a high pitched "whirring" call. Littlejohn's Tree-frogs make a series of drawn out "creep-creeep-creeeep" noises and the Jervis Bay Tree-frog's call sounds like two or three high pitched squeals.

Above: Verreaux's Tree-frogs (pictured), Jervis Bay and Littlejohn's Tree-frogs mostly breed during winter and early spring.

the FACTS!

THE VICTORIAN FROG favours swamps, wet and dry eucalypt forests and grasslands and, as its name suggests, is only found in central Victoria.

VERREAUX'S TREE-FROG lives in wet and dry eucalypt forests, alpine grasslands and bogs, as well as coastal swamps and lagoons in eastern Australia from South-East Queensland to eastern Victoria.

WET EUCALYPT FORESTS, coastal heathlands and swamplands in coastal southern New South Wales and adjacent parts of Victoria are home to the Jervis Bay Tree-frog (below).

LITTLEJOHN'S TREE-FROG tadpoles have been observed swimming in schools and eating the eggs of Verreaux's Tree-frogs, and of their own species.

THE REVEALED FROG can be found in a range of habitats from coastal swamps to mountain forests. It is often found near still water. There are three isolated populations of this frog in north-eastern, mid-eastern and south-eastern Queensland.

LITTLEJOHN'S TREE-FROGS live in the eucalypt forests, woodlands and heaths of coastal southern New South Wales and eastern Victoria.

Anura — Hylidae

Cryptic tree-frogs
— green & brown disguises

Order: Anura
Family: Hylidae

When it comes to camouflage, brown and green are favourite colours for frogs, enabling them to remain almost invisible among plants and rocks and in patches of light and shade.

TWO SPECIES of green and brown tree-frogs living in subtropical and temperate parts of coastal eastern Australia use their colouring well to avoid predators.

The Cascade (or Pearson's) Tree-frog *(Litoria pearsoniana*, below) and the Leaf Green Tree-frog (*Litoria phyllochro*a) are light green to dark olive, or sometimes fawn. Each has a pale whitish or gold stripe along the snout and a dark stripe along the sides. Colouring varies between individuals and at different times of the year.

Cascade Tree-frogs live in rainforest gullies and wet eucalypt forests — often in mountainous areas. Leaf Green Tree-frogs occur around coastal lagoons, streams, swamps and waterholes. Each of the frogs grow 3–4 cm long.

the FACTS!

THE ALPINE TREE-FROG is the only tree-frog (family: Hylidae) that occurs above the winter snowline on mainland Australia.

THE AMOUNT OF GREEN on the backs of Alpine Tree-frogs varies. Some are almost entirely green with a few narrow dark markings (below), while others have a complicated pattern of green, brown and black (above).

THE HILLS ARE ALIVE

There are two populations (subspecies) of the Verreaux's Tree-frog and each is a different colour. *Litoria verreauxii verreauxii* (Verreaux's Tree-frog) is widespread in lowland areas of New South Wales, Victoria and southern Queensland. It ranges from brown to reddish and fawn. *Litoria verreauxii alpina* (Alpine Verreaux's Tree-frog), inhabits mountain grasslands and bogs in the Australian Alps. The two frogs look almost exactly the same, except that *alpina* has broad patches of green. No one is quite certain why the colour difference occurs, but it might reflect differences in vegetation or temperature in the frogs' environments.

Conservation Watch
The Alpine Tree-frog and Peppered Frog are Vulnerable. Others have undergone substantial population declines. Threats include loss of habitat, climate change and fungal disease.

BLUE MOUNTAINS TREE-FROG

Coastal woodlands, eucalypt forests and heaths in southern New South Wales and eastern Victoria support populations of the Blue Mountains Tree-frog (*Litoria citropa*). The female of this species scatters her eggs as she lays them by kicking the water with her hindlegs. The eggs then spread out and sink to the bottom.

GLANDULAR FROG

The Glandular Frog (*Litoria subglandulosa*) is found from the Granite Belt of South-East Queensland to Northern New South Wales. Its golden-brown tadpoles are known to drag themselves along the bottom with their mouths, while feeding. The adult frog is green to olive-brown on the back and has a gold stripe from the nostrils down the side of the body. A broad dark stripe runs beneath the golden one and sometimes there is a white stripe on the upper lip.

Above: The Blue Mountains Tree-frog grows to 6 cm and is light brown with dark flecks. The frog's legs, along with part of its back and the sides of its head and body, are bright green with a dark streak.

DAVIES' TREE-FROG

The Davies' Tree-frog (*Litoria daviesae*) and the Glandular Frog were thought to be the same species until recently being split. They are hard to tell apart, but they occur in different localities and this may help to identify them. The Davies' Tree-frog is found between the Hunter and Hastings Rivers in Northern New South Wales.

TASMANIAN TREE-FROG

The Tasmanian Tree-frog (*Litoria burrowsae*) has the distinction of being the most southerly of all Australian tree-frogs. It inhabits rainforests, alpine sedgeland and moors in Tasmania and is often found around the edges of ponds among reeds and grasses. The mating call of a Tasmanian Tree-frog is said to resemble the honking of a goose.

Above: Glandular Frogs are found along permanent streams in forest above 300 m. These frogs breed in shaded pools where the stream does not flow as strongly.

the FACTS!

CASCADE TREE-FROGS are often found near fast-flowing rocky streams; they shelter under rocks, logs and leaf litter.

THE BREEDING CALL of the Cascade Tree-frog (below) is a sharp "yiiik chik chik" sound. Males call during spring and summer on warm nights along watercourses and still pools after rain. These frogs lay clumps of 360–730 eggs, which they attach to rocks, debris and aquatic plants. Their tadpoles are dark brown with fine gold flecks and are usually found in shallow water at the sides of streams and pools.

THE LEAF GREEN TREE-FROG'S mating call sounds like "erk… erk…erk". Males call during spring, summer and autumn from vegetation above the water. Eggs are laid in loose clusters attached to sticks and leaves, near the edges of streams. Tadpoles are small and range from dark to light golden-brown. These tadpoles are also sprinkled with gold and they are not very strong swimmers.

THE PEPPERED FROG (*Litoria piperata*) inhabits open forests and wet eucalypt forests on the New England Tableland.

Anura — Hylidae

Small tree-frogs
— heard but not seen

Order: Anura
Family: Hylidae

Australian tree-frogs are a large and diverse group. Very few species are found over large areas of Australia. It is more common to find a group of closely-related frogs that live in different regions of the continent.

ONE RATHER UNREMARKABLE small brown tree-frog has the distinction of being Australia's most common and widespread frog. The Red Tree-frog (*Litoria rubella*) occurs over all but the most southern edge of the Australian mainland and Tasmania, from the coast to the arid interior. They are often found hiding in holes and crevices and beneath stones and bark. Buildings, fences and other man-made structures are also favoured shelters.

the FACTS!

THE RED TREE-FROG has had many different common names including the Naked Tree-frog, Purple Tree-frog, Ruddy Tree-frog and Desert Tree-frog.

ONCE THE EGGS are fertilised, a female Bleating Tree-frog (below) kicks the water with her hindlegs to scatter the eggs which then sink to the bottom. Tadpoles are dark brown and are active at all depths, but are often seen at the surface.

THE BLEATING TREE-FROG is found in coastal wetlands, rainforests, wet and dry eucalypt forests, gardens and urban bushland along the coast and highlands of southern Queensland and New South Wales. It is cream-brown to grey-brown with three stripes down the middle of its back. The backs of the thighs, armpits and groin are usually lemon-yellow, especially in males. Bleating Tree-frogs grow to 4.5 cm.

Above: Red Tree-frogs vary from grey and red-brown to fawn on the back, with some darker flecks and a dark spot on each hip. A dark band runs from the snout along the side of the body.

BLEATING & BUZZING TREE-FROGS

The closest relatives of the Red Tree-frog are the Bleating Tree-frog (*Litoria dentata*) and Buzzing Tree-frog (*Litoria electrica*), but neither of these occurs as widely, or is as common.

Bleating and Buzzing Tree-frogs are named for the high pitched mating calls they produce, which are said to be painful to the human ear, especially when large numbers of males gather to open a chorus.

Left: Bleating Tree-frogs (pictured) make a rising "creeee", while Buzzing Tree-frogs make a noise like a high voltage electric arc.

Small tree-frogs
— sedgefrogs

Order: Anura
Family: Hylidae

Conservation Watch
The Wallum Sedgefrog is listed as Vulnerable and is threatened by habitat loss due to urban expansion in coastal regions.

Sedgefrogs often advertise their presence as the garden is being hosed. These small, sharp-snouted tree-frogs emit squeaky calls and are one of the few species of frogs that will bask in the sunlight.

SEDGEFROGS ARE DIVIDED INTO THREE GROUPS of species: the Slender Tree-frog (*Litoria adelaidensis*), "sharp-snouted frogs" and "dwarf tree-frogs". At 6 cm, the Slender Tree-frog is the largest, and is found only in the south-west of Western Australia.

SHARP-SNOUTED FROGS

Sharp-snouted frogs are found mainly in New Guinea, but there are two Australian species. The Javelin Frog (*Litoria microbelos*, right) is the most widespread and occurs across wetter parts of tropical northern Australia. The Long-snouted Frog (*Litoria longirostris*), is found only in the rainforests of the McIlwraith Range on Cape York Peninsula. Both are small brown frogs that grow to 2–2.5 cm.

Left: Northern Sedgefrogs are not only common around gardens. Large numbers occur around the lakes, lagoons and wetlands of tropical northern Australia.

DWARF TREE-FROGS

Gardeners in northern and eastern Australia often encounter small green to fawn tree-frogs hiding in foliage, sitting on leaves, or even clustered in small groups at the bases of broad-leafed plants. Tropical gardeners are likely to be finding the Northern Sedgefrog (*Litoria bicolor*) while those along the east coast will be seeing the Eastern Sedgefrog (*Litoria fallax*).

Not all sedgefrogs are common and familiar. The Wallum Sedgefrog (*Litoria olongburensis*) only occurs in the coastal lowlands, or wallum country, of southern Queensland and Northern New South Wales. Cooloola Sedgefrogs (*Litoria cooloolensis*) are restricted to acidic lakes and lagoons between Fraser Island and North Stradbroke Island, Queensland.

Left: Eastern Sedgefrogs will readily respond to changes in air pressure and humidity by making a high-pitched squeaking call.

the FACTS!

SEDGEFROGS are usually seen hiding in low plants and among sedges along ponds and dams. During the non-breeding season, some species appear to seek shelter high in the tree canopy. As the first spring and summer rains approach, they can often be heard calling from their high retreats.

SEDGEFROGS commonly perch in the stems of sedges, grasses and twigs. These perches are easily disturbed, so the frogs are able to detect the movement of possible threats. In addition, these thin perches do not obscure possible threats that approach from below. Sedgefrogs that have long, very narrow snouts, like the Wallum Sedgefrog, have a very good forward and downward field of vision.

THE JAVELIN FROG lives in creeks, lagoons and paperbark swamps where it often hides among leaf litter and reeds.

"ACID FROGS" live in the coastal woodlands and heaths, sandy freshwater lakes and lowland rainforests of South-East Queensland and Northern New South Wales. In these areas, the water is stained brown with tannin and has a high acid content.

THE SLENDER TREE-FROG lays eggs in loose clumps attached to plants or just on the surface of the water. The tadpoles are brown with a pair of white stripes that run down the body.

Conservation Watch

The Armoured and Mountain Mistfrogs are Critically Endangered.

Waterfall frogs
— life in the rapids

Order: Anura
Family: Hylidae

Mountain streams are a haven for frogs; here they are protected from one of their deadliest enemies — fish. The waterfalls and cascades that form as streams descend to lower altitudes and prevent most fish from entering the upper reaches of streams. These places are home to some very special frogs that seem to like life in the "fast-lane".

the FACTS!

THE COMMON MISTFROG (above and below) is the most widespread of the three mistfrogs. It also occurs at lower elevations than the others.

THE AUSTRALIAN LACE-LID (*Nyctimystes dayi*) is a large-eyed tree-frog named for the appearance of its lower eyelid, which is patterned with a lacework of fine gold, or thick pearly pigmented lines. It grows to 5 cm and lives in the highlands and adjacent foothills of the Wet Tropics. Lace-lids are often seen perched on rocks and plants at the side of fast-flowing streams.

THE MATING CALL of the Waterfall Frog is a short harsh growl. Like many torrent-dwelling frogs, males of this species have lost their vocal sac, as a mating call is hard to hear above the roar of fast-flowing water.

MALE WATERFALL FROGS have small spines on their thumbs and chests so they can cling to a female and not get swept away in the swift current.

THE TADPOLES of the Mountain Mistfrog have been observed burrowing into loose sand under rocks in stream beds.

IN RAINFOREST AREAS, rocky streams are often permanently wet and mossy. Climbing pads on the fingers and toes of tree-frogs help them clamber over these slick surfaces, so it is not surprising that a number of species have adapted to life in rocky streams and are found nowhere else.

The Waterfall or Torrent Tree-frog (*Litoria nannotis*), Armoured Frog (*Litoria lorica*), Cape Melville Tree-frog (*Litoria andiirrmalin*), Common Mistfrog or Creek Frog (*Litoria rheocola*) and the Mountain Mistfrog or Nyakala Frog (*Litoria nyakalensis*) are all stream-dwellers from the rainforests of north-east Queensland.

Above: More than twenty species of lace-lids (*Nyctimystes* spp.) occur in New Guinea and all have distinctively patterned eyelids.

STRONG SWIMMERS

Waterfall frogs are usually seen on boulders beside or behind waterfalls and near cascades. They are powerful swimmers and will not hesitate to leap into fast-flowing water to escape danger. Waterfall and mistfrogs occur in the highlands and adjacent foothills of the Wet Tropics, with the exception of the Cape Melville Tree-frog which is found only in the mountains after which it is named, on Cape York Peninsula. Most are coloured in various shades of grey, olive green or brown to blend with the surrounding rocks.

Left: The Waterfall Frog can be grey to olive-green to almost black on its back with lots of darker mottling. It grows to a body length of 6.5 cm.

Torrent tree-frogs
— going with the flow

Order: Anura
Family: Hylidae

Conservation Watch
The Waterfall Frog, Spotted Tree-frog, Australian Lace-lid and Common Mistfrog are Endangered.

Anura — Hylidae

Although it has the greatest diversity of stream-dwelling frogs, Queensland's Wet Tropics is not the only place to find frogs that have adapted to fast-flowing waters. In other areas these are known as "torrent frogs".

SOME STREAM-DWELLING TREE-FROGS look like typical tree-frogs. However, others are less conventional — they have pointed snouts and very long hindlegs. The Stony-creek Frog (*Litoria wilcoxii*, right) and its close relatives from eastern Australia are arguably the best known of these stream-dwellers but similar-looking species can be found in other parts of northern Australia.

Above: The Rockhole Frog (*Litoria meiriana*) lives on rock outcrops, rocky hills and gorges near waterholes and creeks in north-west Australia. It is small (2 cm) and fast which gives it the ability to "skip" across the surface of water in a series of bounces.

the FACTS!

THE MASKED FROG'S preference for rocky habitats has led to it also being known as the Masked Rock Frog or Masked Cave Frog. Males call in summer from rock faces near water. The tadpoles are chocolate-brown with a pair of long gold stripes. They often swim in groups.

THE SPOTTED TREE-FROG (*Litoria spenceri*) is a stream-dweller that looks like a typical tree-frog. It lives in wet and dry eucalypt forests, often near rocky streams and creeks in the highlands of central Victoria and nearby parts of the Australian Capital Territory. Breeding occurs in summer and the mating call is a "warrrk…cruk..cruk..cruk..cruk" sound. The eggs are laid in a single clump under rocks, in 10-30 cm of flowing or still water.

ROCKY AREAS with permanent water and waterfalls provide many moist shelter sites that are ideal for frogs. It is common to find stream-dwelling frogs clustering, like these Rockhole Frogs (below), behind waterfalls and in rock crevices for shelter. They will also cling to rocks at or just above the waterline.

Above: The Masked Frog's liking for rocky habitats has led to its alternate common names — Masked Rock Frog or Masked Cave Frog.

COLOURFUL CHORUSES

The males of some stream-dwelling frogs, such as the stony creek frogs and the Masked Frog (*Litoria personata*), become brightly coloured during the breeding season. Lesueur's Frog (*Litoria lesueuri*), Stony-creek Frog and Jungguy Tree-frog (*Litoria jungguy*) males are bright lemon-yellow. Masked Frog males are yellow with dark mottling.

Rocky streams are often very noisy, so frogs that breed there often rely on visual display rather than call. Distinctive breeding colours are likely to help females find the right mates.

Rocket-frogs
— over the top

Order: Anura
Family: Hylidae

Rocket-frogs are among the champion "hoppers" of the frog world. Other species of tree-frogs have quite short hindlegs, but the ground-dwelling rocket-frogs have powerful hindlegs that can propel them a long way in a single hop.

ROCKET-FROGS ARE EASY TO RECOGNISE because of their long legs, pointed heads and thin streamlined bodies. They have no need to climb, so the discs on the tips of their fingers and toes are tiny. Although rocket-frogs can be found across northern and eastern Australia, different species inhabit different areas and habitats.

Rains that refresh wetlands and swamps produce numerous temporary waters that are welcomed by rocket-frogs. Males form loud noisy choruses where they make rapid "wak-wak-wak" calls and this is why some naturalists refer to them jokingly as "racket frogs". Although the calls differ slightly, the sound of a rocket-frog is unmistakeable.

the FACTS!

IN NORTHERN AUSTRALIA, frogs are often used as bait by anglers, who refer to their victims as "barra (barramundi) frogs". The most prized species are various rocket-frogs, especially the Broad-palmed Frog (*Litoria latopalmata*) and Bumpy Rocket-frog (*Litoria inermis*). However, the use of frogs as bait is illegal because all species are protected native fauna.

MANY THOUSANDS OF FROGS are killed each year as they cross roads on wet nights while moving to breeding areas. The dead frogs provide a feast for a host of scavengers and predators.

TORNIER'S FROG (*Litoria tornieri*) is restricted to the Kimberley Region of Western Australia and the western parts of the Top End of the Northern Territory.

THE BUMPY ROCKET-FROG is also known as Peter's Frog or the Floodplain Frog and is found from the north of Western Australia to the Queensland-New South Wales border.

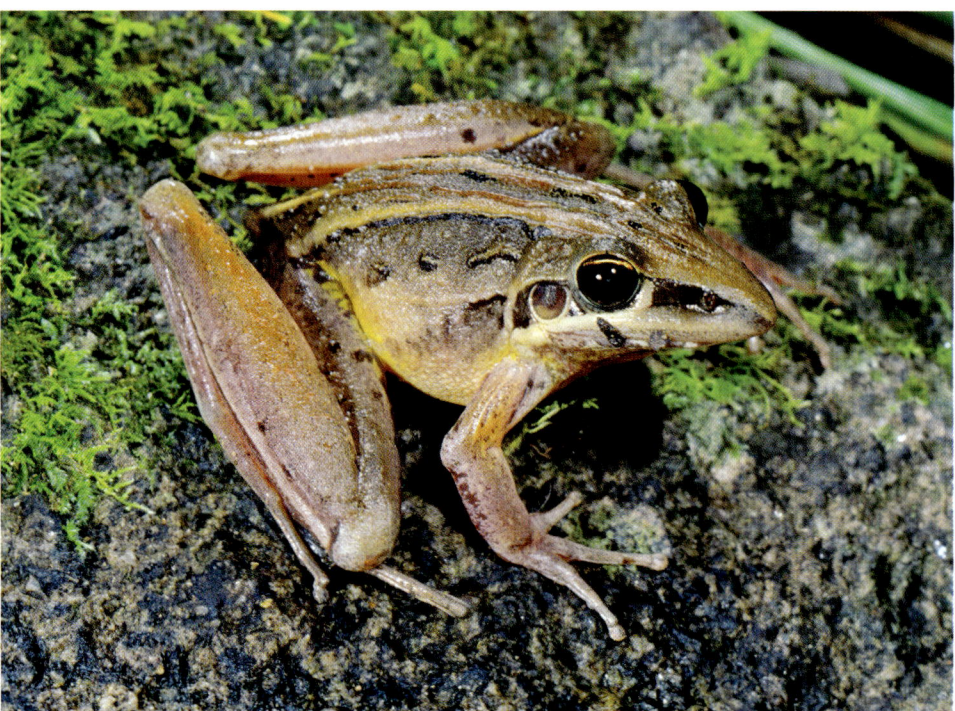

Above: The Striped Rocket-frog is slender and brown with two long lines of dark warts, ridges and skin folds along its back. A wide dark stripe runs from the snout across the face and the backs of the thighs are yellow with dark brown lines.

SUMMER BREEDERS

Spring and summer rains bring rocket-frogs out in droves, even if the area where they live is dry for most of the year. These are the frogs that are briefly seen as they cross roads on rainy nights in just one or two hops. Rocket-frogs are sharp-eyed and wary. At the slightest disturbance they will crouch and prepare to leap for safety.

Males call from the ground around water and may be partly hidden in grass or leaf litter. The Bumpy Rocket-frog (*Litoria inermis*), which is perhaps the plainest and least remarkable species, has the most distinctive call. It makes a series of low growls or chuckles then switches to a very intense "meeeek, meeek, meek" repeated frequently.

Conservation Watch
All of the rocket-frogs are considered to be Secure.

TWO OF A KIND

The most well known rocket-frog is the Striped Rocket-frog (*Litoria nasuta*), which is widespread across northern and eastern Australia. It grows to 5 cm and inhabits open forests, swamps, streams, ponds, waterholes and flooded grassy areas.

The Freycinet's Frog, or Wallum Rocket-frog, (*Litoria freycineti*) is similar to the Striped Rocket-frog, except that its back is patterned with irregular dark blotches, warts and skin folds arranged in rows. It lives in woodlands, open forest, heaths and temporary swamps in coastal lowlands of southern Queensland and Northern New South Wales.

Below: The Freycinet's Frog grows to 2.5 cm. This rocket-frog is found in sandy and sandstone heaths, and breeds in swamps, streamside pools and temporary puddles.

the FACTS!

THE BROAD-PALMED ROCKET-FROG (above) is widespread across southern Queensland and Northern New South Wales, the Northern Territory and South Australia.

ONE OF THE MOST MYSTERIOUS Australian frogs is the Green-thighed Frog (*Litoria brevipalmata*, below) from southern Queensland and Northern New South Wales. This frog will suddenly appear in large numbers after heavy spring and summer rains only to disappear just as quickly. Green-thighed Frogs may not be observed again for years.

STRONG MARKINGS

The Bridled Frog, or Tawny Rocket-frog, (*Litoria nigrofrenata*) is the largest and most striking species with its pale fawn or brown back and contrasting black sides. It grows to 5 cm and is found only in Tropical North Queensland.

Other rocket-frogs are smaller (3–3.5 cm long) and drab coloured. Rocket-frogs' groins and the backs of their thighs are yellow with dark brown spots, bars and other markings. They occur in open forests, woodlands and open areas on floodplains, but are also found near creek beds, dams, swamps and marshes.

Rocket-frog eggs are laid in clusters near the surface and either float freely on the surface or attach to vegetation. Outside the breeding season, rocket-frogs can often be found well away from a water source. They usually hide in various natural and artificial nooks and crannies and under rocks, logs and other debris.

Left: The Pale Frog (*Litoria pallida*), also known as the Pallid Rocket-frog or Peach-sided Rocket-frog, is found across northern Australia.

THE MATING CALL of the Striped Rocket-frog is a rapid "ik-wik-wik".

AS THEY DEVELOP, rocket-frog eggs sink to the bottom of the water body where they eventually hatch.

THERE MAY BE AS MANY as 450 individual eggs in a Bridled Frog egg cluster, while large clusters of Broad-palmed Rocket-frogs may contain between 300–350 eggs. Most rocket-frog egg clusters contain between 30–100 eggs.

Bell frogs
— shining gems

Order: Anura
Family: Hylidae

Several groups of Australian tree-frogs have adapted to life on the ground. Among them are the spectacular bell frogs, which are brightly coloured in shades of green, gold and bronze, with a splash of blue in the groin and across the backs of the thighs.

BELL FROGS LIVE in permanent freshwater swamps, lagoons, ponds and dams. They prefer water bodies that have thick vegetation around the edges and floating plants on the surface. Like most other frogs, breeding occurs after rain during the spring and summer months.

Some people assume that a "pretty" animal will make a sweet sound or call. This is generally untrue across the animal kingdom and is certainly untrue of the beautiful bell frogs. Their calls have been likened to growls, quacks and even a motorcycle changing gears!

Bell frogs are large (7–8.5 cm), robust frogs. With one exception, bell frogs occur across temperate southern parts of mainland Australia and northern Tasmania.

Above: Dahl's Aquatic Frog is most likely to be seen around extensive freshwater wetlands, swamps and billabongs in tropical northern Australia.

the FACTS!

THE DAHL'S AQUATIC FROG (*Litoria dahlii*, above) is the only bell frog that occurs in the northern tropics, and at 7 cm it is also the smallest of the group. It is not as brightly coloured as other species and its call is like a soft bark. Despite these differences, it still looks like a bell frog. The Dahl's Aquatic Frog lives in the woodlands of northern Australia. It breeds during January and February and probably at other times during summer after rain.

MALE BELL FROGS start calling after rain in spring, summer and autumn while floating among vegetation in water. Bell frogs lay clusters of eggs that are floating, submerged or attached to vegetation in shallow water. Like rocket-frog eggs, the eggs sink as they develop. The tadpoles of some species take anywhere between three and fifteen months to develop into young frogs.

SPECIES DECLINES

Bell frogs, like most large frogs, will eat whatever they can catch and overpower. Their diet consists mainly of insects, but if they have the opportunity, they will eat small animals including other frogs. Bell frogs themselves are not immune to predators such as birds and fish. The introduced mosquitofish (*Gambusia* spp.) are voracious predators of frog eggs and tadpoles. These fish have been implicated in the massive population declines of some bell frogs that were once very common. This serves as a warning that even if an animal is considered "common", there is no guarantee it will be safe for all time.

Left: Green and Golden Bell Frogs were once regarded as common. Serious declines in numbers now mean that it is a species at risk.

Conservation Watch
The Yellow-spotted Tree-frog is Endangered. The Green and Golden Bell Frog and Southern Bell Frog are Vulnerable. Threats include a fungal disease, climate change, loss of habitat, an introduced predatory fish and water pollution.

Anura — Hylidae

NOT SO COMMON

Two species that have declined throughout their former range are the Southern Bell Frog (*Litoria raniformis*, right) and the Green and Golden Bell Frog (*Litoria aurea*). Both were once common throughout eastern New South Wales and adjacent parts of Victoria.

The Southern Bell Frog has a four-part call beginning with a series of grunts: "crok-crok" followed by a slow "craw-craw-crawk". The Green and Golden Bell Frog sounds similar. Its call starts with a slow *craw-craw-crawk* and is followed by some short grunts.

The Green and Golden Bell Frog, which grows to 8.5 cm, became famous when building began on the Sydney 2000 Olympics site. A breeding population was found in an old abandoned quarry on the site and an environmental campaign was launched to save the colony.

GO WEST

The Western Green and Golden Bell Frog (*Litoria moorei*) can be found around suburban lakes, lawns and backyard ponds in Perth, Western Australia. Its natural habitat is swamps, watercourses, flooded melaleucas and areas of dense reeds. Breeding occurs in summer, after rain. Males spend many nights calling to attract a mate. Their eggs are laid as a floating mass attached to vegetation.

Left: The Western Green and Golden Bell Frog is well-known and popular in Western Australia.

"MOTORBIKE FROGS"

In some areas, bell frogs are even known as "Motorbike Frogs" because of their breeding calls. The mating call of the Western Green and Golden Bell Frog from the south west corner of Western Australia is a long, low growl. Another species from the same area, the Spotted-thighed Frog (*Litoria cyclorhyncha*), sounds like a motorbike accelerating then changing gears. The first part of the call is drawn out and the second part is a short burst of sound.

Left: The Spotted-thighed Frog is gold-brown with irregular green blotches.

the FACTS!

BELL FROGS are one of the few frogs that will bask in the sun and it is thought their green and golden colouring may help camouflage them at such times.

THE SOUTHERN BELL FROG (below) and the Western Green and Golden Bell Frog both grow to 8 cm.

THE YELLOW SPOTTED TREE-FROG (*Litoria castanea*) is only found on the New England Tableland of Northern New South Wales and its mating call is a series of grunts that sounds like the hum of a distant motorbike. This species grows to about 8 cm.

Anura — Hylidae

Greenstripe frog
— racing stripes

Order: Anura
Family: Hylidae

Most Australian tree-frogs, whether they are "true" tree-frogs or ground-dwellers, live in wetter parts of Australia. Many are only found in the narrow coastal strip, but one genus, Cyclorana*, is found in drier areas and even arid parts of the continent.*

CYCLORANA SPECIES ARE BURROWERS and typically only emerge from below ground after heavy rains and flooding. Unlike other tree-frogs, they are solidly built with deep, rather than flat, bodies. They resemble the burrowing pobblebonks and spadefoots/shovelfoots of the family Limnodynastidae.

There are four distinct types of *Cyclorana*: the striped burrowing, snapping, water-holding and collared frogs. Each represents a slightly different solution to life in the often harsh dry climates that exist in the heart of continental Australia.

Above: Striped Burrowing-frogs grow to 6.5 cm. They can be brown, olive-brown or green with darker flecks and blotches. Most have a yellowish or light green stripe down the spine and a dark streak along the snout, through the eye and on to the sides where it breaks up into dark spots.

GREENSTRIPE BURROWER

The Striped Burrowing-frog, or Greenstripe Frog, (*Cyclorana alboguttata*, right) lives in woodland, grassland and cleared areas in dry parts of Queensland, New South Wales and the Northern Territory. It favours low-lying and alluvial areas where temporary pools and shallow flooding occur after heavy rain. Striped Burrowing-frogs are voracious predators and often feed on smaller frogs that are breeding alongside them. They also eat insects, other invertebrates and occasionally small ground-dwelling lizards such as geckoes.

the FACTS!

MALE STRIPED BURROWING-FROGS advertise breeding and their reappearance above ground with a mating call that sounds like quacking ducks. These frogs mainly breed during spring and summer in flooded ditches and claypans, marshes, paddocks and dams. Their eggs are laid in clumps near the edge of the water, near where the males have been calling from.

ALTHOUGH THE STRIPED BURROWING-FROG is mainly associated with low rainfall inland regions, they are occasionally found in wetter areas along the coast. For example, small populations of Striped Burrowing-frogs have been found in Brisbane in South-East Queensland. Sadly, many of these colonies have now disappeared as their habitats have been swallowed up by continuing urban expansion.

IF MUSCLES ARE UNUSED for long periods of time, they will become weak and decrease in size. This process is known as muscular atrophy and it could be a problem for the many frogs that remain inactive for long periods of time, sometimes years. However, studies of the Striped Burrowing-frog have shown that even after nine months of inactivity, the muscles of this frog remain unchanged. The same is likely to be true of other frogs.

Snapping-frogs
— greedy hunters

Order: Anura
Family: Hylidae

Conservation Watch
The Striped Burrowing-frog and snapping-frogs are considered to be Secure.

Most frogs are voracious predators. Although they mainly prey on insects and small invertebrates, a large frog will eat whatever animal it can overpower and force down its throat. It is not uncommon to find large tree-frogs occasionally eating small birds and mammals.

THE TWO SNAPPING-FROG species are ravenous predators that frequently dine on other frogs. Victims are manipulated and positioned with the front feet before they are forced headfirst down the snapping-frog's throat.

The Northern Snapping-frog or Giant Frog (*Cyclorana australis*) ranges across the north of Australia from the Roper River in the Northern Territory to the Gulf of Carpentaria in Queensland. The Eastern Snapping or New Holland Frog (*Cyclorana novaehollandiae*) occurs throughout the drier parts of Queensland and adjacent parts of New South Wales. Both frogs look similar, growing to around 10 cm and both favour floodplains, open forests, woodlands and grasslands; they are seen only after heavy rains.

Above: The ranges of the Northern Snapping-frog and Eastern Snapping-frog (below) overlap in north-west Queensland, where occasional hybrids between the two species are found.

the FACTS!

A SNAPPING-FROG will spend the long dry season buried underground. It stores water in its bladder and in pockets under the skin. Evaporation is reduced by a cocoon of shed skin. Once the rains arrive this frog breaks through the cocoon and digs its way to the surface.

STUDIES HAVE SHOWN that Striped Burrowing-frogs and snapping-frogs are close relatives. The same studies have shown that *Cyclorana* spp. are more closely related to the bell frogs than any other group of Australian tree-frogs.

AN ADULT NORTHERN SNAPPING-FROG can be grey, brown, fawn or dull pink and sometimes has green patches on its back. The backs of the thighs can range from flesh coloured to dark blue. The skin on the back has some low warts and two longitudinal skin folds. Juvenile snapping-frogs are often bright green.

THE EASTERN SNAPPING-FROG is pale grey, brown or yellowish with dark brown flecks and blotches. Juveniles are often bright green or have green blotches. The backs of the thighs are grey or blue-tinged. The skin on the back is smooth or may have small warts.

LURKING SNAPPERS

Snapping-frogs will lurk around breeding ponds to feed on the males of smaller frogs, such as marsh and rocket-frogs, as they gather to form breeding choruses. Male frogs are more likely to be victims because of their numbers and choice of call sites on the ground at the water's edge.

It is not unusual to find that the snapping-frogs are breeding in the very same ponds at the same time.

Water-holding frogs
— drought cheaters

Order: Anura
Family: Hylidae

Water is a scarce and valuable resource in the arid interior of Australia. Animals and people that live there must find ways of conserving water and making the most of rains and floods.

FOR MOST OF THE YEAR, there is little sign of any frog life in Australia's dry interior, except for those that lurk around bores, rainwater tanks and other sources of moisture. But after heavy rains during spring and summer, large numbers of frogs will suddenly appear as if by magic and the cool night air carries their mating songs both far and wide.

The Water-holding Frog (*Cyclorana platycephala*) is a burrowing inland frog that has special adaptations to allow it to live in desert conditions. When it comes to the surface after rain, it has an aquatic lifestyle. The frog absorbs large quantities of water through its skin and stores this in its tissues, particularly in the bladder, where it can be re-absorbed later. As soon as conditions start to dry out, the Water-holding Frog burrows into the soil to protect itself and avoid dehydration.

When underground, the frog forms an external, almost waterproof cocoon of mucous and sloughed skin. This cocoon reduces its water loss at a rate comparable to a surface-dwelling lizard.

Right and below: Water-holding Frogs range in colour from dull grey to dark brown to green.

A FAST LIFE

The Water-holding Frog is found in claypans, ditches and pools and often spends time underwater feeding on insects, tadpoles and smaller frogs. It has very small eyes that are positioned near the top of its flat head. This enables the frog to remain submerged with only its eyes and nostrils clear of the water.

Males call from the water or beside pools, ditches and swamps. The mating call is a slow "maw-w-w" sound, a little like a small motor. The eggs are laid in clumps with more than 500 eggs being laid at one time. Tadpoles are dull gold and wriggle their whole body when they swim. They develop quickly before the water dries up.

the FACTS!

MOST SPECIES OF CYCLORANA, such as the Wailing Frog (below) and the Hidden-ear Frog (above) will breed in almost any temporary pools and are often found calling and breeding in roadside puddles.

ONCE A WATER-HOLDING Frog locates a suitable breeding pond, it is likely to stay there until it has to return underground. However, some can be highly mobile and capable of moving distances of around 200 m in an hour.

SMALL ANIMALS, such as desert amphibians, reptiles and rodents and other small mammals, are known as "evaders" because they avoid high temperatures and reduce water loss by sheltering in shady rock crevices, underground burrows or shade. The ultimate evaders are considered to be desert frogs, including *Cyclorana* spp., which spend most of the year dormant and cocooned inside a burrow.

THE WATER-HOLDING FROG was well known to Aboriginal people who used to dig up the dormant frogs and squeeze them, in order to collect and drink the water stored in the frog's body.

Collared frogs
— water seekers

Conservation Watch
The Water-holding Frog and all of the collared frogs are considered to be Secure.

Order: Anura
Family: Hylidae

The biggest group of *Cyclorana* spp. are the collared frogs. These small squat frogs take their name from the pale, collar-like band that crosses the back of their necks.

THEY INHABIT WOODLANDS and grasslands and are usually found near temporary ponds, swamps, ditches, low-lying areas, claypans and creeks after rain. Males call while floating in water, or from bare ground and in grass tussocks along the edges of water. Their mating calls include bleating, barking, moaning or mooing sounds.

Right: The Knife-footed Frog is also known as the Grassland Collared Frog and Desert Collared Frog; it is about 5 cm long.

SMOOTH AND WARTY

Most collared frogs grow to 4–5 cm long, but apart from the pale "collar" and sometimes a pale stripe along the back, their appearance varies. Most collared frogs have light and dark markings on their backs, but some have smooth skins and others have a warty appearance. The back of the Rough Frog (*Cyclorana verrucosa*) is perhaps the roughest of all, being covered in warts and long folds of skin. The smallest species is the Little Frog (*Cyclorana manya*) from Cape York Peninsula, which only reaches 3 cm.

Above: The Wailing Frog makes a call like a bleating sheep.

the FACTS!

THE LONG-FOOTED FROG (below) has an unusual mating call, a long, drawn out sound, which is said to resemble the mooing of cattle.

THE HIDDEN-EAR FROG lives in open grasslands with clay soils. Its mating call is a loud bark that is frequently repeated.

THE WAILING FROG lives in open grassland and gets its common name from the sound of its call — a repeated crying sound.

WAILING FROGS have been found gorging themselves on shield shrimps (*Triops* spp.) in shallow temporary ponds.

ACROSS THE COUNTRY

More than nine species of collared frogs are found in arid and semi-arid areas of Australia. Three occur in the east — the Short-footed Frog (*Cyclorana brevipes*), Little Frog and Rough Frog. The Knife-footed Frog (*Cyclorana cultripes*) is a central Australian species, and the Daly Waters Frog (*Cyclorana maculosa*) is from northern Australia. The four remaining species — Hidden-ear Frog (*Cyclorana cryptotis*), Long-footed Frog (*Cyclorana longipes*), Main's Frog (*Cyclorana maini*) and Wailing Frog (*Cyclorana vagita*, left) — are from Western Australia.

Tusked Frog
— getting big-headed

Anura — Limnodynastidae

Conservation Watch
The Tusked Frog has disappeared or declined in some parts of its range, but is regarded as Secure.

Order: Anura
Family: Limnodynastidae

Appearances can be deceiving, even in the animal world. At first glance, the Tusked Frog (Adelotus brevis) is an unimpressive muddy-looking frog. But, on its underbelly a striking black and white pattern with red colour flashes is revealed.

TUSKED FROGS ARE UNUSUAL ground-dwelling frogs. The male Tusked Frog is not only larger than the female, a rare thing among frogs, but it also has a huge head and two "tusks". The "tusks" are tooth-like projections on the lower jaw. They fit into special holes in the roof of the mouth and are only seen when the mouth is open.

It has a mottled dark brown back with dark blotches covered with small warts. This nondescript colour pattern is broken up by bright red patches in the groin area and on the back of the legs, and a black and white belly.

the FACTS!

TUSKED FROGS are found in coastal areas and adjacent highlands along the southern coast of Queensland and Northern New South Wales. The frogs inhabit rainforests, wet eucalypt forests and open grasslands and are often found under logs, stones or leaf litter near puddles, creeks and ponds.

THE MATING CALL of the Tusked Frog is a slow, repeated "rook". Males call from concealed sites in or near water in spring and summer. They are highly territorial and aggressive towards each other.

THE BRIGHT BLACK AND WHITE BELLY and patches of red in the groin and on the legs are a feature only of male Tusked Frogs.

Above: Tusked Frog males grow to 4.5 cm and females to 3.5 cm. They usually have a butterfly-shaped marking between the eyes, and the arms and legs have dark bands.

COMPETING MALE Tusked Frogs will wrestle and use their tusks to bite the opponent around his throat.

IN WARM CONDITIONS during summer, Tusked Frog tadpoles take 50 days to hatch.

NEST-BUILDERS

Male Tusked Frogs (above and right) make nests in concealed sites under leaf litter, vegetation, logs or rocks at the edges of pools or streams. They also use water-filled yabby burrows and will even breed in the water-filled holes left by cattle hooves.

The female lays hundreds of eggs in a white floating foam nest which the male guards. Tadpoles are dark brown to black and sometimes have a small cream patch on the tip of the snout.

Fletcher's Frog
— killer tadpoles

Conservation Watch
Fletcher's Frog is considered to be Secure.

Anura — Limnodynastidae

Order: Anura
Family: Limnodynastidae

Fletcher's Frog (Lechriodus fletcheri) is sometimes known as the "sandpaper frog" because of the rough skin on its back. The frog also produces a powerful skin toxin as a defence against predators.

FLETCHER'S FROGS inhabit the rainforests and wet eucalypt forests of South-East Queensland and Northern New South Wales. They live in and around forest pools or streams and may be found among leaf litter on the forest floor and in hollows among tree roots.

The frogs breed during the warmer months of the year in shallow pools of water or streams. They will even breed in water-filled ruts created by motor vehicles along forest tracks. The mating call is a purring "gar...r..r..up" sound.

Up to 600 eggs are laid in a foam nest and the tadpoles are pale or dark brown with gold specks. The tadpoles are voracious feeders that will become cannibalistic — the weaker, smaller ones becoming prey for their larger siblings.

Right: Male Fletcher's Frogs call while floating in the water or sitting in leaf litter.

SHARP RIDGES

A Fletcher's Frog can be fawn to reddish-brown or black on its back and may have a few darker markings. Its arms and legs have dark coloured bars and there is a dark stripe from the nostril through the eye to the shoulder.

The frog has several distinctive ridges on its body. These run from the eye to the shoulder and along the lower back and legs. There is also an X-shaped ridge between the shoulders. Fletcher's Frogs grow to 5 cm.

Left: Like many frogs that live on the rainforest floor, the Fletcher's Frog is patterned to blend with the leaf litter that carpets the forest floor.

the FACTS!

FLETCHER'S FROG has feet with dark undersides, so is sometimes known as the Black-soled Frog.

IN NEW GUINEA there are three other species of *Lechriodus*. It is the only genus of Australian water or ground frogs — which are in the families Limnodynastidae and Myobatrachidae — that has more species in New Guinea than Australia.

THE REMAINS OF *LECHRIODUS* species have been discovered at the Riversleigh fossil site in north-west Queensland.

Anura — Limnodynastidae

Mountain frogs
— splendid isolation

Order: Anura
Family: Limnodynastidae

Fossils show that some frog species have been part of the Australian environment for a very long time and that they were once more widespread than they are now. As the climate warms and becomes drier, high cool mountain tops have become island-like refuges: the only habitat left for some species.

the FACTS!

LOVERIDGE'S FROGS' EGGS are laid in a small jelly-like mass in two layers with the majority of eggs in the top layer and a few beneath. Tadpoles are cream to yellow-brown in colour and develop in the jelly mass like other species.

THE BAW BAW FROG grows to 4.5 cm long. It is dark brown with scattered dark flecks and light patches on its back. Two large (parotoid) glands above its shoulders are dark brown or black. The belly is cream or yellow with brown flecks.

MALE BAW BAW FROGS call during late spring from burrows in sphagnum moss or depressions under rocks and logs. The mating call is a complex and variable "clunk" or "uk…uk…uk" repeated at intervals.

THE MATING CALL of the Sphagnum Frog is a low growling "gur-r-r-r-r-r". Males call from burrows under rocks and logs, in sphagnum moss or under trees.

THE PUGH'S SPHAGNUM FROG (*Philoria pughi*) lives in cool temperate and subtropical mountain rainforests. Males call with a low, slow grunt (late winter to summer) from nest sites under leaf litter and rocks. Large sticky eggs are laid in small, water-filled cavities.

MOUNTAIN OR SPHAGNUM FROGS (*Philora* spp.) are known from the famous Riversleigh fossil site in Queensland. They lived there when Australia's climate was much wetter than at present. If mountain frogs are survivors from prehistoric times, it is appropriate that they are often found living near another survivor that has found sanctuary in the mountains: Southern Beech trees (*Nothofagus* spp., right).

The Baw Baw Frog (*Philoria frosti*, above) is known only from Mt Baw Baw in Victoria. It lives in sheltered mountain gullies at 1080–1560 m elevation and is often found under rocks and logs near streams or in sphagnum bogs. Females lay 50–100 large eggs in small foam nests in damp depressions in the ground. The nest breaks down into a watery jelly and the dark brown tadpoles hatch into this jelly where they remain until they metamorphose into tiny frogs.

Conservation Watch

The Baw Baw Frog is Endangered. Threats include logging, damage to habitat, recreational activities and climate change. The remaining species are considered to be Secure.

RED AND YELLOW MOUNTAIN FROG

The Red and Yellow Mountain Frog (*Philoria kundagungan*, right) occurs along the Scenic Rim of South-East Queensland. It lives in rainforest and can be found in damp leaf litter, under logs and stones or under rocks and boulders that line soaks and small creeks. This mountain frog may be red, black or yellow and it has two dark V-shaped patches near the back legs. A black stripe runs from the nostril through the eye to the shoulder, and its belly is smooth and bright yellow. The frog grows to 3 cm and its mating call is a low, slow "ork". Males call during late winter through to summer from nest sites. The eggs are laid in small water-filled cavities.

the FACTS!

PUGH'S SPHAGNUM FROG is a brightly coloured frog of the Gibraltar Range in Northern New South Wales. It grows to 3 cm. Its colour pattern is maroon, orange, or orange with black patches and it has a yellow belly, and yellow sides with maroon flecks. A black stripe runs from the nostril through the eye to the shoulder.

A RELATED SPECIES, the Richmond Range Sphagnum Frog (*Philoria richmondensis*), from Northern New South Wales, is also strongly patterned in brown, bronze, orange or orange with dark marks and speckles. It grows to 2.7 cm and has similar habitat preferences and breeding biology to Pugh's Sphagnum Frog.

LOVERIDGE'S FROG grows to 3 cm and is found in mountain forests along the Queensland-New South Wales border. This frog is dependent on high soil moisture levels, and is found only where ground-water is always close to the surface.

THE SPHAGNUM FROG (*Philoria sphagnicolus*) occurs mainly on the New England Tableland of Northern New South Wales. It can be cream, yellow, orange, red or black, with darker flecks and blotches. It has dark bands along the snout, the sides of the body and each hindleg. The belly is white. This frog grows to 3.5 cm and inhabits Southern Beech forests, wet eucalypt forests and sphagnum moss beds. It is found in moist soil or moss burrows and under rocks and logs beside streams.

LOVERIDGE'S FROG (*Philoria loveridgei*) is found in Southern Beech forests, wet eucalypt forests and rainforests above 750 m. It is also known as the Masked Mountain Frog because it has a dark band that runs from the snout through the eye to the shoulder. It is mostly brown. Loveridge's Frogs burrow into moist soil or moss beside streams. Their mating call is a low, slow "ork" or "orp". Males call from their burrows from late spring to early summer.

Marsh-frogs
— hardy croakers

Order: Anura
Family: Limnodynastidae

*Marsh-frogs (*Limnodynastes *spp.) are hardy, adaptable creatures able to live in swamps, marshes and even drains and puddles. Some species are equally at home in natural or disturbed habitats.*

THESE GROUND-DWELLING FROGS are found in Australia, New Guinea and on some Torres Strait Islands, and there are two main forms. The striped or spotted marsh-frogs have flat bodies and pointed snouts and the burrowing banjo frogs or "pobblebonks" are squat with deep bodies. All have a raised pale stripe running below the eye to the arm.

the FACTS!

THE SPOTTED MARSH-FROG, or Spotted Grass Frog (*Limnodynastes tasmaniensis*, below) is the most commonly encountered marsh-frog. It is found throughout the eastern half of Australia to Tasmania in habitats ranging from wet coastal woodlands to the dry interior. It is light brown to olive-green with irregular darker spots and blotches and a pinkish, yellow or white stripe down the middle of the back.

THE BARKING or Long-thumbed Frog (*Limnodynastes fletcheri*) is a similar species from inland southern Australia. It grows to 5 cm and lives in water-covered grassy areas and around the banks of large lakes and rivers, sheltering under rocks and logs, and in yabby burrows.

Above: Striped Marsh-frogs are light brown or grey-brown with darker brown stripes and they frequently have a pale stripe running down the middle of the back. Their arms and legs are scattered with irregular dark spots and bands and the underside is white.

STRIPED MARSH-FROG

Most people are probably more familiar with the loud, monotonous "tok" call of the Striped Marsh-frog (*Limnodynastes peronii*) than the frog itself. The call is repeated at regular intervals and can be loud enough to disturb the sleep of anyone nearby. The Striped Marsh-frog can live almost anywhere, from garden ponds to drains and ditches and seems to be able to tolerate polluted water. During the day, it hides under logs, stones and leaf litter. Striped Marsh-frogs grow to around 6.5 cm and are found along the east coast of Australia to Tasmania.

Left: Male Striped Marsh-frogs begin to call on land before moving to shallow water to continue their calling.

Conservation Watch
All of the flat-bodied marsh-frogs are considered to be Secure.

Anura — Limnodynastidae

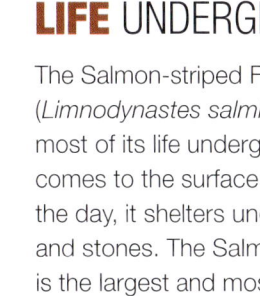

LIFE UNDERGROUND

The Salmon-striped Frog (*Limnodynastes salmini*) spends most of its life underground and only comes to the surface after rain. During the day, it shelters under logs, loose bark and stones. The Salmon-striped Frog is the largest and most attractive of the flat-bodied marsh-frogs, growing to 7 cm. It is also known as Steindachner's Frog.

Left: The Salmon-striped Frog is brown to grey with dark spots and blotches, and three pink to orange-red stripes on its back — two on each side and one down the middle. Another orange-red stripe runs from below the eye to the top of the arms.

TROPICAL MARSH-FROGS

The Marbled Marsh-frog (*Limnodynastes convexiusculus*), Carpenter Frog (*Limnodynastes lignarius*) and Flat-headed Frog (*Limnodynastes depressus*) are tropical species from northern Australia. The Marbled Marsh-frog is the largest of the three at 5.5 cm. It lives in woodlands and swampy areas and calls from under vegetation or debris, or from the flooded burrows of other animals.

Left: Marbled Marsh-frogs are grey, brown or dark olive with lots of large dark blotches.

FLAT-HEADED FROG

The Flat-headed Frog has exactly that — a noticeably "flat" head, which has prominent, jutting upper eyelids. Its breeding call sounds a bit like a short burst of machine-gun fire. The Flat-headed Frog (4 cm) is only found in the Keep River area on the Northern Territory–Western Australian border. The Carpenter Frog also has a flat head and a very large ear membrane (tympanum). It lives in the sandstone hills and gorges of north-western Australia.

Left: The Carpenter Frog grows to 5 cm and has a rich chocolate-brown back with dark blotches and often patches of yellow or white.

the FACTS!

ALL MARSH-FROGS lay their eggs in white frothy clumps that float on water. Breeding females have a flange along the side of their fingers, which they use to beat the water, air and jelly of their eggs together to create the foam.

THE BARKING or Long-thumbed Frog has a pink or purplish patch on the back of each upper eyelid.

FEMALE STRIPED MARSH-FROGS usually lay up to 1000 eggs. The frogs breed during the warmer months of the year.

THE SALMON-STRIPED FROG occurs from the central coast of Queensland into the northern interior of New South Wales.

THE MATING CALL of the Marbled Marsh-frog is a loud, high pitched repeated honk.

Anura — Limnodynastidae

Banjo frogs
— marsh musicians

Order: Anura
Family: Limnodynastidae

The squat, dark-faced, chunky burrowing banjo frogs or "pobblebonks" are named for their calls, which the human ear interprets as short, resonant "plonks" or "bonks". A large chorus of these frogs may actually sound like the strumming of a banjo.

POBBLEBONKS RESEMBLE OTHER BURROWING FROGS more than they do their closest relatives, the flat-bodied marsh-frogs. They also differ from other marsh-frogs in that they have a large swollen gland on the upper surface of their lower hindleg.

Above: Pobblebonks live in forests, woodlands and cleared areas, usually near dams, swamps and ponds that are surrounded by dense vegetation.

the FACTS!

THE EASTERN BANJO FROG is one of only two species of Australian frogs that can be divided into distinctive populations or subspecies. The other is the Verreaux's Tree-frog.

THERE ARE FIVE SUBSPECIES of Eastern Banjo Frog which differ in size, amounts of webbing on the feet and colour pattern.

THE WESTERN BANJO FROG (*Limnodynastes dorsalis*) of Western Australia is separated from its nearest relatives by the vast treeless expanse of the Nullarbor Plain. Western Banjo Frogs live near swamps, streams and dams. Most breeding occurs in winter and the mating call is a repeated single "plonk" or "bonk". Males call from hidden sites while sitting in the water. The eggs are laid in a large frothy mass which is usually attached to vegetation.

PREDATORS OF BANJO FROGS often discard the legs and their associated glands, indicating that the glands contain toxins. Extracts taken from the tibial glands of the Scarlet-sided Pobblebonk, Eastern Banjo Frog and the Giant Banjo Frog have been found to contain unique chemical compounds.

NEW ZEALAND'S RARE and endemic *Leiopelma* frog species were threatened by the deliberate introduction of Australian Eastern Banjo Frogs into the Waitakere Ranges and Auckland. These introduced frogs have since been located and eradicated in a conservation effort to help the *Leiopelma* species.

THE "QUEENSLAND" FROG

The Scarlet-sided Pobblebonk (*Limnodynastes terraereginae*) is also known as the Northern Banjo Frog or Northern Bullfrog. It occurs in eastern Queensland and drier parts of Northern New South Wales. Its Latin species name, *terraereginae*, actually means "Queensland".

Scarlet-sided Pobblebonks are colourful frogs. Their backs are grey or brown with darker blotches and sometimes a pale stripe down their spine. There is a slightly raised cream to reddish-orange stripe from under the eye to the arm, and a similar coloured stripe along each side of the body. The upper arms have a red patch, the belly is white or pale yellow and the groin is yellow and red. Pobblebonks grow to 4.5 cm.

Conservation Watch
All of the banjo frogs are considered to be Secure.

Anura — Limnodynastidae

THE EASTERN BANJO FROG

The Eastern Banjo Frog (*Limnodynastes dumerilii*) is found in the cooler regions of southern Australia and Tasmania and, at 7 cm, it is larger than its subtropical cousin (the Scarlet-sided Pobblebonk). It is also known as the Grey-bellied or Eastern Pobblebonk, or Bullfrog. Although it is bigger, the Eastern Banjo Frog is less colourful, being grey, olive-green, or dark brown to black, with dark marbling, blotches or flecks. A pale stripe runs from under the eye to the arm and the belly is white — sometimes mottled with grey.

The Eastern Banjo Frog inhabits woodlands, rainforests, heathlands, farmlands and grasslands. It is commonly seen after rain near dams and other bodies of still or slow-moving water. The mating call is a single "plonk" or "bonk" repeated at intervals.

Above: The Eastern Banjo Frog may have areas of yellow or cream along its sides but lacks any trace of scarlet or orange.

BIGGEST OF ALL

The Giant Banjo Frog or Giant Bullfrog (*Limnodynastes interioris*) is the largest of all of the banjo frogs, growing to 9 cm long. This spectacular large burrowing frog occurs in central parts of New South Wales. It favours dry country and lives in woodlands, shrublands and sandy areas, but is usually only seen after heavy rain.

The Giant Banjo Frog varies from pale yellow and fawn to red-brown and has a few small dark flecks and spots. Broad bands of coppery-orange extend along the sides of the body. The rest of the sides are black with scattered bluish-white spots. A cream, yellow or orange raised stripe runs from below the eye to the arm.

Males call from burrows in the banks of dams and pools throughout most of the year, except during hot, dry summers.

Left: The mating call of the Giant Banjo Frog is less banjo-like and more like a deep "plunk".

the FACTS!

FOAM NESTS are constructed during mating. The female paddles with her front feet making air bubbles which pass along her belly and mix with the eggs and jelly to create the foam.

800-1100 EGGS may be laid by Giant Banjo Frogs in their large foamy egg nests at the edge of dams, ponds and ditches. The egg masses are often partly concealed. The tadpoles take at least six months to metamorphose.

MALE EASTERN BANJO FROGS call throughout most of the year from burrows at the water's edge or while afloat among vegetation. Calling is more intense after heavy rain and males will sometimes congregate in large numbers.

Burrowing frogs
— disappearing act

Order: Anura
Family: Limnodynastidae

Most burrowing frogs are seldom seen and a chance encounter is a matter of being in the right place at the right time after rain. As the rain falls and water begins to seep into the soil, it acts as a trigger for the frogs to become active. It is possible to hear some of these burrowers calling before they reach the surface.

THERE ARE MANY GROUPS OF BURROWING FROGS. Some, like *Opisthodon* spp., are common and widespread. They may even turn up in rural and urban backyards after rain. Others, like *Heleioporus* spp., are much less common and are often only found in particular habitats.

Above: Burrowing Frogs (*Opisthodon* spp.) can be encountered in many habitats from sandy desert and floodplains to coastal sand dunes.

Above: Ornate Burrowing Frogs lack the venom glands of a toad and have a smooth white belly and a more rounded shape.

ORNATE BURROWING FROG

The squat Ornate Burrowing Frog (*Opisthodon ornatus*) is sometimes mistaken for a small toad. It has warty skin on its back and its colour varies from reddish, to dark brown, to pale grey. It can also have dark spots, blotches or other markings. There is often a butterfly or U-shaped light patch on the back behind the eyes. The legs and arms are also barred or spotted with dark bands and blotches. Ornate Burrowing Frogs live in a wide range of habitats from the wet eucalypt forests of the coast to the dry woodlands of northern and eastern mainland Australia.

the FACTS!

LIKE THE ORNATE BURROWING FROG, Spencer's Burrowing Frog has a range of colours and markings and a similar butterfly or U-shaped light patch on the back behind the eyes.

FEMALE ORNATE BURROWING FROGS (below) may lay more than 1500 eggs at a time. The tadpoles grow rapidly (25–90 days depending on conditions) and often prey on smaller tadpoles. Ornate Burrowing Frogs grow to 4.5 cm.

MALE GIANT BURROWING FROGS call in spring and autumn from burrows in the banks of creeks or dams. They either construct their own burrow or use one that has been made by a yabby. Females lay their eggs in foamy masses inside the male's burrow or in dense vegetation. Tadpoles are eventually flushed into the creek when it rains.

FOAM NESTS are constructed by four genera of Australian Frogs: *Adelotus, Lechriodus, Limnodynastes* and *Opisthodon*. The eggs are suspended in the foam just above the water line where it is warmest. This may accelerate the development of the eggs.

Conservation Watch
The Giant Burrowing Frog is Vulnerable. All other species of burrowing frogs are considered to be Secure.

Above: The mating call of Spencer's Burrowing Frog is a rapid "hau-hau-hau-hau" sound.

DESERT BURROWING FROG

Spencer's Burrowing Frogs (*Opisthodon spenceri*) are mainly found in sandy areas near creeks and rivers. This species breeds after rain and has an accelerated development. The eggs are laid in a foam nest that breaks down within 24 hours to form a thin frothy layer.

The tadpoles can complete their development in around 40 days. This species is also known as the Desert Burrowing Frog or Spencer's Frog.

BURROWERS NEAR AND FAR

Frogs of the genus *Heleioporus* are squat and robust with broad heads; they are mostly black, brown and grey. Most species occur in the south-west of Western Australia and only one, the Giant Burrowing Frog (*Heleioporus australiacus*), is found on the east coast.

Some frogs are closely associated with particular soil types, habitats or topography and the Giant Burrowing Frog is one of these. It is restricted to sandstone areas of the Hawkesbury region in New South Wales where it lives around sandy creek beds.

Above: The Giant Burrowing Frog calls like an owl, "oo…oo…oo".

DIFFERENT CALLS

The five Western Australian species of *Heleioporus* have different calls. The Western Marsh-frog (*Heleioporus barycragus*) makes a low, owl-like hoot and the call of the Western Spotted Frog (*Heleioporus albopunctatus*) is a slow, high pitched wavering "coo-ooo-ooo". The Plains Frog (*Heleioporus inornatus*) sounds like "woop-woop-woop", while Sand Frogs (*Heleioporus psammophilus*) have a "put-put-put-put" call. As its name suggests, the Moaning Frog (*Heleioporus eyrei*) makes a moaning sound.

Above: Western Spotted Frog males call from their burrow, which is also where the pair mate.

the FACTS!

WESTERN SPOTTED FROG males may construct a breeding burrow which may be more than 1 m long. The eggs are large and laid in a frothy mass where they develop until hatching, which occurs when the burrow is flooded.

THE WESTERN MARSH-FROG is likely to be found along temporary watercourses that flow in winter over clay or granite.

WESTERN AUSTRALIAN HELEIOPORUS spp. like the Sand Frog (below), breed in autumn and early winter. Males call from burrows where the pair will mate.

THE WESTERN SPOTTED FROG prefers sandy swamps and creeks, while the Plains Frog prefers peaty swamps and bogs in wet forest.

SAND AND MOANING FROGS live where there are sandy or peaty swamps and bogs.

Spadefoots & shovelfoots

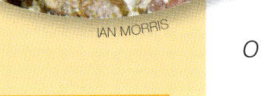

Order: Anura
Family: Limnodynastidae

Some frogs are so similar in appearance, habitat and distribution, they can only be identified by scientific examination. The ten species of Neobatrachus *frogs are like this. They are hard to distinguish from each other, but easy to tell apart from other burrowing frogs.*

THESE TUBBY FROGS are 4–5 cm long and they have a black, hard raised lump on the inside sole of each hindfoot. These structures act like little shovels when the frogs are burrowing. These frogs are known as spadefoots and shovelfoots.

Spadefoot frogs are found across drier regions of Australia with most in Western Australia, the Northern Territory and South Australia. Most species live in grasslands, woodlands, farmlands and cleared areas.

Right: The Northern Burrowing Frog (*Neobatrachus aquilonius*) lives mainly in spinifex and grasslands.

the FACTS!

NORTHERN SPADEFOOT FROGS (*Notaden melanoscaphus,* above) live in grasslands and eucalypt woodlands with clay soils. The mating call is a loud "whoop", made by males while floating amongst grasses in shallow water during the December to March wet season. Females lay over 1000 eggs at once in long lines around water plants.

THE PAINTED FROG or Mallee Spadefoot Toad (*Neobatrachus pictus,* below) is found in the south-east of South Australia and western Victoria.

THE DESERT SPADEFOOT FROG lives in arid sandy areas and is only seen after rain. Males call, with a low "whoop", repeated slowly, in large choruses mostly during summer rains. Breeding takes place in shallow ponds and flooded areas. Tadpoles develop in sixteen days.

THE TRILLING FROG (*Neobatrachus centralis*) is the most widespread spadefoot species; it occurs from the far west of Queensland and New South Wales into Western Australia.

BREEDING CALLS

Males of most *Neobatrachus* spp. call while floating in still water. They make high or low-pitched trilling calls, low-pitched hums or moans. The Goldfields Bullfrog (*Neobatrachus wilsmorei*) makes a short "plonk" and the Shoemaker Frog (*Neobatrachus sutor*) is named after its call — a short tap repeated regularly that sounds like a shoemaker tapping nails into a shoe.

Above: Kunapalari Frogs (*Neobatrachus kunapalari*) favour clay and sandy soils in the Western Australian wheat belt.

Breeding occurs after heavy rain mainly during summer, but some of the Western Australian species will also breed into autumn and winter. Most breed in pools, marshes, flooded paddocks, ditches and pools in creeks. Humming Frogs (*Neobatrachus pelobatoides*) will also breed in pools on granite outcrops.

The males of some species develop black spines over their backs during the breeding season. Eggs are laid in long chains that form loose clumps around plants in the water. Females lay approximately 1000–1400 eggs.

Conservation Watch

All of the spadefoot burrowing frogs are considered to be Secure.

Anura — Limnodynastidae

COLOURFUL CHARACTER

The four small species of *Notaden* frogs are also known as spadefoots or shovelfoots. These frogs burrow backwards into the soil in a corkscrew fashion. In contrast to other Australian burrowing frogs, these frogs have small heads and fat bodies. *Notaden* spp. feed mainly on ants and termites and will lurk alongside trails of these insects to feed. They have warty skin glands and can produce a sticky, white toxic mucus for defence.

The most colourful member of this group is the Crucifix Toad (not actually a "true toad") or Holy Cross Frog (*Notaden bennettii*, above). This bright yellow, olive or green frog has a cross-shaped pattern of black, red, white and yellow spots across its back.

The Crucifix Toad is often found in black soil along the western slopes of the Great Dividing Range to the floodplains of inland Queensland and New South Wales.

the FACTS!

THE MATING CALL of the Northern Spadefoot Frog (below) is an owl-like "whoop-whoop". Breeding males call while floating in shallow pools. The eggs are laid in long chains that wrap around water plants and they hatch after four days. The bright brown tadpoles feed on plants and soft-bodied insects.

WEIGEL'S TOAD lives in open woodlands and is often associated with hummock grasses and rocky outcrops.

SPADEFOOT FROGS feature unusual eyes. They have vertical pupils and shiny silver or gold irises.

SUDELL'S FROG (*Neobatrachus sudelli*, below) lives in woodlands, grasslands and disturbed areas in southern Queensland, New South Wales and Victoria. It is also called the Meowing Frog.

CLOSE FAMILY

The remaining three *Notaden* spp. are found in northern Australia. The Northern Spadefoot Frog, also known as the Brown Shovelfoot or Brown Orb-frog (*Notaden melanoscaphus*), ranges from the Kimberley region of Western Australia to around Townsville in Queensland. It is dull olive-brown or red-brown with several dark blotches — one on the head, one on each shoulder, one in the middle of the back and one on either side of the pelvic area. The area between these large blotches is yellowish to brown with irregular flecks of yellow, black and red. It is similar in size to the Crucifix Toad; both grow to 5.5 cm.

The Desert Spadefoot Frog (*Notaden nichollsi*) is found in central Australia and in parts of Western Australia. It is similarly coloured in shades of brown, grey or olive with low dark warts and white, yellow and red spots. White or yellow spots are also scattered along the sides of the body; it reaches 6 cm.

The third species, Weigel's Toad (*Notaden weigeli*), is restricted to the northern Kimberley region of Western Australia. At 7 cm it is the largest of the *Notaden* species. Weigel's Toad is reddish-brown with faint olive blotches. There are small orange lumps with white tips on the back and the belly is grey.

Left: The entire breeding cycle of the Northern Spadefoot Frog takes two months to complete.

Day-frogs
& tinkerfrogs

Order: Anura
Family: Myobatrachidae

In recent years, frog populations have been declining worldwide. Scientists are not sure of the exact reasons, but it is likely to be a combination of circumstances. Australia has not been immune.

TWO AUSTRALIAN SPECIES, which are now believed to be extinct, are the Sharp-snouted Day-frog (*Taudactylus acutirostris*) and the Southern Day-frog (*Taudactylus diurnus*). These frogs have not been seen in the wild for almost three decades. *Taudactylus* are ground-dwelling frogs of the mountain rainforests and they can also be found in fast-flowing rocky streams. Most frogs are nocturnal, (active after dark), but three species are diurnal — finding the daylight hours more to their liking.

the FACTS!

AUSTRALIAN RAINFORESTS do not have as many frog species as rainforests in other parts of the world. This is due to the small size and the limited distribution of Australian rainforests which are now found mainly along the east coast. However, many of the frogs that are found in Australian rainforests do not occur anywhere else.

THE SHARP-SNOUTED DAY- FROG was first described in 1916. The remaining species of *Taudactylus* were discovered and described between 1966 and 1986.

THE SMALL DARK TADPOLES of the Sharp-snouted Day-frog had large rounded mouths that helped them to cling onto rocks in fast-flowing water.

LIKE OTHER TORRENT-DWELLING FROGS, Southern Day-frogs would dive into water when alarmed and hide under rocks or in submerged leaf litter until danger had passed.

Above: Sharp-snouted Day-frog males called from among the rocks and litter close to streams all year round. Females laid 25–40 large eggs in a gelatinous clump on the undersides of rocks, at or below the waterline in running creeks.

SHARP-SNOUTED DAY-FROG

The most distinctive *Taudactylus* was the Sharp-snouted Day-frog (left). It was olive-brown with a black face and sides. A pale fold of skin separated the dark sides from the brown back. The legs were olive-brown with dark cross-bars and the belly was greyish-white with black flecks. The groin and undersides of the arms and legs were yellow. The snout was pointed and protruded beyond the lower jaw.

The Sharp-snouted Day-frog grew to 3 cm. It had two types of calls. One was a high-pitched metallic tink…tink…tink, repeated several times in quick succession and the second was a scratchy "eek…eek…eek chirp".

Conservation Watch

The Sharp-snouted Day-frog and Southern Day-frog are presumed to be Extinct. The Eungella Day Frog and Tinkling Frog are Endangered. The Pleione's Torrent Frog is Vulnerable.

SOUTHERN DAY-FROG

The Southern Day-frog from South-East Queensland was found in and around slow flowing streams and was often seen hopping over rocks, through leaf litter, or perched on low waterside plants.

It was grey or brown with darker mottling and had a dark H-shaped mark on the back between the shoulders and the arms. The belly was cream or bluish and the frog grew to about 3 cm.

Left: The Southern Day-frog, also known as the Mount Glorious Torrent Frog, was only found at Mt Nebo, Mt Glorious and in the Blackall–Conondale Ranges near Brisbane in South-East Queensland.

THE TINKERS

Some secretive species of *Taudactylus* are more likely to be heard than seen. Their calls sound like the tinkling of tiny "fairy bells". This has lead to them being known as "tinkerfrogs". Like the day-frogs, the tinkerfrogs live in rainforests and other wet forests in the mountains of eastern Queensland. All species are at risk. They include the Tinkling Frog (*Taudactylus rheophilus*), the Eungella Tinkerfrog or Liem's Frog (*Taudactylus liemi*), and the Pleione's Torrent Frog (*Taudactylus pleione*).

Pleione's Torrent Frog only occurs in wet mountain forests at Kroombit Tops to the west of Gladstone in southern Queensland. It is grey with dark blotches and an X-shaped patch between the shoulders. The arms and legs have black cross-bars.

Below: There is little or no sign of the Pleione's Torrent Frog. Only when rains approach in summer do the males start calling from deep in rock crevices before forming choruses.

the FACTS!

THE MATING CALL of the Eungella Day-frog (*Taudactylus eungellensis*) is a soft "cluck-cluk-cluck-cluck" repeated in short bursts. The eggs are large and are laid in clumps of 30–50 under rocks in water. The tadpoles are orange-brown, with a distinctive V-shaped marking behind the eyes.

THE TINKLING FROG grows to 3 cm and inhabits the mountain forests of north-east Queensland. It is often found under rocks and logs beside fast-flowing streams as well as seepages and soaks.

EUNGELLA DAY-FROGS are similar to Southern Day-frogs in their behaviour and choice of habitat. They are restricted to the Eungella National and Finch Hatton Gorge National Parks west of Mackay in Queensland. The frogs grow to 3.5 cm and are yellowish-tan to dark brown with darker mottling. They have a dark X-shaped mark on the back between the shoulders.

BREEDING MALE EUNGELLA TINKERFROGS sometimes call from yabby holes in creek banks.

MALE TINKLING FROGS call all year round from under rocks, boulders and leaf litter. Their egg masses have not been observed, but females carry around 35–50 large eggs.

THE EUNGELLA TINKERFROG is grey-brown with a dark pattern in the shape of a lyre (musical instrument) on its back and a dark brown triangular patch on the head.

EUNGELLA DAY-FROG males call with greatest intensity during spring and summer and communicate to each other by flicking and waving their legs, head bobbing, and making distinctive hops.

Marsupial frogs
— good parents

Conservation Watch
The Marsupial Frog is Secure.

Order: Anura
Family: Myobatrachidae

Frogs have evolved many ways of caring for their young. Frog species around the world have about 30 different ways of laying eggs and about ten different ways of caring for their eggs and young. All of these strategies have evolved to ensure the survival of as many of the young as possible.

SOME FROGS CARRY THEIR TADPOLES WITH THEM in special pouches until they are ready to make their way in the world. These pouched frogs are often known as "marsupial frogs". Australia's Marsupial Frog (*Assa darlingtoni*) inhabits the southern beech forests and subtropical rainforests of the mountains of South-East Queensland and Northern New South Wales. This small frog, which is about 3 cm long, lives in leaf litter or among rocks and fallen logs. It is grey to red-brown and some specimens also have an upside-down V-shaped marking on their backs.

Above: The Marsupial Frog is also known as the Pouched Frog and Hip-pocket Frog.

the FACTS!

MARSUPIAL FROG TADPOLES are about 1.5 cm long. When hatched, they are white, but later change to brown stippled with dark brown or black. These tadpoles only have a rudimentary fin because they do not need to enter water.

IT IS BELIEVED MARSUPIAL FROG TADPOLES may breathe by absorbing oxygen from the blood-vessel-rich skin in the male's pouch.

THE CALL OF THE MARSUPIAL FROG is a series of fast, high-pitched "chit-chit-chit-chit" sounds. Males call from leaf litter, rock piles and debris on forest floor in spring and summer.

MATING OCCURS IN SMALL, concealed depressions in the ground.

THE EGG MASSES of Marsupial Frogs are about 1–3 cm across and contain 8–20 eggs. In large clutches, the eggs are laid in two layers and take 11–12 days to hatch. During this time, they are nourished by their yolk-filled stomachs. Metamorphosis takes 60–80 days.

MARSUPIAL FROGS do not need water to breed, but they do need very moist conditions such as wet leaf litter and damp soil. The tadpoles stay in the pouch until they are fully developed frogs.

SPECIALIST BREEDERS

The female Marsupial Frog lays her eggs in a jelly clump on the ground and both sexes guard them. Just before the eggs hatch, the male climbs among the eggs and coats himself in the jelly. This allows the tadpoles to glide over his body and wriggle into the pockets of skin near his hips using their tails. Any tadpoles that fail to reach the pouch are doomed to die.

Rheobatrachus
— platypus frogs

Order: Anura
Family: Myobatrachidae

Conservation Watch
Both species of *Rheobatrachus* are presumed to be Extinct.

In 1973, a zoologist from the University of Queensland described a frog he had discovered in a rainforest creek in the mountains north of Brisbane about a year before. The unusual frog was fully aquatic and closely resembled an odd aquatic frog (*Barbourula busuangensis*) from the Philippines in South-East Asia.

AT THE TIME it was not known that the Southern Gastric-brooding Frog (*Rheobatrachus silus*) had an exceptional way of caring for its tadpoles, or that it would be extinct within the next decade. Female Southern Gastric-brooding Frogs raised their tadpoles in their stomach — during which time they did not eat.

Above: Northern Gastric-brooding Frogs were pale brown with darker blotches. The undersides of the arms, legs and lower abdomen were bright yellow. The rest of the belly was white to brown.

HERE TODAY, GONE TOMORROW…

Above: If disturbed, Southern Gastric-brooding Frogs dived into the water and hid under rocks or in debris on the bottom.

There were two species of gastric brooding frogs. The Northern Gastric-brooding Frog (*Rheobatrachus vitellinus*) was described as a new species in 1984 and became extinct soon after. The last one was seen in the wild in March 1985.

The Southern Gastric-brooding Frog, also known as the Southern Platypus Frog, grew to 5 cm and varied from black to olive-brown with darker blotches. It lived in rocky mountain streams and rarely ventured far from water, often remaining submerged with only its eyes and nostrils exposed. The last individual was seen in the wild in September 1981.

the FACTS!

THE MATING CALL of the Southern Gastric-brooding Frog was a rising "eeeeh…eeeeh". Males called from the water's edge mainly during summer. The eggs were large and it is presumed that the female swallowed them once they had been fertilised. The tadpoles developed in her stomach nourished on their egg yolk until they were regurgitated soon after they had metamorphosed. The female stopped secreting gastric juices and did not feed while she was carrying the young.

THE NORTHERN GASTRIC-BROODING FROG also had an aquatic lifestyle inhabiting fast-flowing rocky rainforest creeks. Its mating call consisted of several loud sharp notes. Males called from the water's edge in summer. Large females reached 8 cm long.

BOTH SPECIES of *Rheobatrachus* had fully webbed toes, an adaption of their aquatic lifestyle.

Barred frogs
— splendid to behold

Order: Anura
Family: Myobatrachidae

There are many attractive frogs in the world, but not all of them are brightly coloured. The barred frogs (Mixophyes spp.), are pleasing to the eye because of their shapes and subtle colouring in shades of brown with black highlights.

SEVEN SPECIES OF BARRED FROGS are found in high rainfall areas of eastern Australia. They are large amphibians with black-banded legs and vertical pupils. Barred frogs live on the floor of wet forests and breed in nearby streams.

Above: A strong swimmer, the Great Barred Frog's mating call is a loud deep, harsh "wark", which can be heard a long way off.

GREAT BARRED FROG

The most common species is the Great Barred Frog (*Mixophyes fasciolatus*), which is found along much of the east coast of mainland Australia. This large frog (8 cm) is grey or brown with a broad dark brown band along the spine and a thin black stripe from the nostril to the ear. The arms and legs have dark cross bars which widen under the legs.

Although it lives mainly in wet forests it can also be found in disturbed areas around dams and ponds.

The female flicks the fertilised eggs out of the water with her hindfeet onto the bank where they stick to rocks and plants. When the tadpoles hatch, they drop back into the water or are washed in by rain. The large dark tadpoles grasp hold of rocks and other surfaces using their mouths.

Left: The Stuttering Frog (*Mixophyes balbus*) is also known as the Southern Barred Frog. It is similar to the Great Barred Frog, but more yellow-grey in colour and lacks a pale upper lip.

the FACTS!

BARRED FROG TADPOLES take many months to metamorphose. It is said that Northern Barred Frog tadpoles may take as much as two years to do so.

THE STUTTERING FROG (below) lives in fast-flowing streams in subtropical and temperate rainforest and wet eucalypt forest along the coast of New South Wales. Its mating call is a short stuttering trill "kook kook kook kra-a-ak… kruk… kruk". The female creates a small hollowed-out nest in shallow flowing water (in the gravel or leaf litter) and lays her eggs in it. The eggs are sticky and either clump together or mix in with the leaf litter or gravel.

THE NEW GUINEA BARRED FROG (*Mixophyes hihihorlo*), is known from a single mountain locality in New Guinea.

TEMPERATURES BELOW 18°C cause Giant Barred Frogs to bury themselves under leaf litter, researchers have found.

Conservation Watch
Fleay's Frog and the Giant Barred Frog are both Endangered. The Stuttering Frog is Vulnerable.

Anura — Myobatrachidae

THE GIANT BARRED FROG

For most frogs becoming a meal for a snake is a real possibility, but not for the Giant Barred Frog (*Mixophyes iteratus*). One of Australia's largest frogs, it is known to occasionally make a meal of frog-eating snakes, including the highly venomous Rough-scaled Snake (*Tropidechis carinatus*). The Great Barred Frog reaches 11.5 cm in body length. It is dark olive to black with irregular dark blotches down the back and has a broad band of dark spots and blotches down the sides.

Left: The Giant Barred Frog has similar habits to the Great Barred Frog, but rarely ventures beyond the edge of the forest. Its mating call is a soft, guttural "ork".

FOREST STRONGHOLD

The wet forests of eastern Queensland are the stronghold for barred frogs and are home to three species that are not found elsewhere.

Fleay's Barred Frog (*Mixophyes fleayi*) lives in streams in the mountains of southern Queensland and Northern New South Wales. It grows to 8 cm and is pale brown with similar markings to other species. The mating call is "ok-ok-ok-ok-ok" and its breeding behaviour is similar to that of the Stuttering Frog.

Left: Fleay's Barred Frog has dark cross bars on its arms and legs, which form a triangular pattern under the legs.

AT HOME IN THE WET

Three species of barred frogs occur in the Wet Tropics of north Queensland. The most common species is the Wet Tropics Barred Frog (*Mixophyes coggeri*) which occurs throughout the region. The remaining two species are only found in the highlands. Northern Barred Frogs (*Mixophyes schevilli*) are found on the Big and Atherton Tablelands as well as Thornton Peak, while Carbine Barred Frogs (*Mixophyes carbinensis*) only occur on the Carbine and Windsor Tablelands.

Left: The Wet Tropics Barred Frog is the only northern species to occur in both the mountains and lowlands.

the FACTS!

BARRED FROGS HIDE (above) during the day under leaf litter or burrow into the loose soil. Their colour patterns help them blend with dry fallen leaves. They emerge at night to forage on invertebrates such as insects and worms. They will occasionally eat small vertebrates such as snakes and other frogs.

MODERATE RAINFALL is the cue for male barred frogs to gather at a few suitable breeding sites around permanent water. If rainfall is heavy, they disperse more widely — probably to take advantage of temporary streams and ponds.

SEVERAL SPECIES OF BARRED FROG have declined in recent decades. In the case of the Giant Barred Frog, numbers have seriously declined in the mountains while lowland populations have been largely unaffected.

NORTHERN AND WET TROPICS Barred Frogs occur together on parts of the Atherton Tableland. The Wet Tropics Barred Frog can be distinguished by the series of dark blotches (rather than a single broad dark band) down the middle of its back and a few dark-edged pale blotches on the back of its thighs.

Gungans
— the little fake toads

Order: Anura
Family: Myobatrachidae

The gungans or toadlets (Uperoleia spp.) are one of the groups of frogs in Australia that seem to multiply constantly. In some areas it is possible to find two or more species living side-by-side.

GUNGANS ARE SMALL, squat, ground-dwelling frogs that superficially resemble tiny toads. They have warty skin with numerous skin glands and there is often a raised gland behind each eye (parotoid gland) and another on the side of the body between the front and hindlegs. However, the toadlets have bright red, orange or yellow on the edges of the hindlegs and groin and the upper side of the forearm may be yellow to fawn.

Above: Toadlets burrow into soil, or shelter under logs, rocks and in leaf litter. The Floodplain Toadlet (*Uperolia innundata*) lives in woodlands and grasslands that flood after monsoon rains.

LOOK-ALIKES

The toadlets are all similar in shape and colour which makes them difficult to tell apart. Fortunately, their mating calls differ. They make two distinct types of calls — "clicks" or "squelches". Toadlets are found across northern and eastern Australia and in the lowlands of New Guinea. They prefer dry eucalypt forests, woodlands, coastal heaths, grasslands and cleared areas that are prone to flooding. A few are habitat specialists. For example, the Tanami Toadlet (*Uperoleia micromeles*) lives in spinifex and mulga sandplains and the Jabiru Toadlet (*Uperoleia arenicola*) lives in sandy soils along the edges of creeks.

Right: The Jabiru Toadlet is pale grey to dark brown with darker flecks and has reddish-orange patches around the groin and behind each knee.

the FACTS!

THE MARBLED TOADLET (*Uperoleia marmorata*) was collected and described in 1841. It has not been recorded since. This toadlet was described as "… black and green marbled, leaving a triangular greenish spot on its forehead, beneath lead colour". It was found in the Kimberley region of Western Australia.

THE NORTHERN TOADLET (*Uperoleia borealis*, top and below) lives in grasslands and breeds in temporary pools after rain. Its call is a short rasping note. The small dark brown tadpoles have a distinctive V-marking between the eyes.

MALE GUNGANS will commence calling from under cover in spring and summer well before they move to their breeding areas. Some individuals may be located at distances of 200–300 m from the nearest permanent water or likely breeding site.

Conservation Watch
The status of the Marbled Toadlet is unknown. All remaining species are considered to be Secure.

Anura — Myobatrachidae

PERHAPS THE MOST WIDESPREAD TOADLET is the Wrinkled Toadlet or Chubby Gungan (*Uperoleia rugosa*, above). This frog occurs over much of New South Wales and the southern half of Queensland. It is brown with dark blotches and usually has a dark triangular patch on its head. The parotoid and other skin glands are large and yellowish. The Wrinkled Toadlet lives in dry forests, woodlands and grasslands. Males call from grass tussocks and leaf litter at the edge of temporary marshes and swamps.

THE STONEMASON TOADLET (*Uperoleia lithomoda*, above) is another widespread species ranging from the Kimberley region of Western Australia to Cape York Peninsula and the Wet Tropics of Queensland. It is grey-brown with darker brown patches and often has a pale cream stripe down the middle of its head. The Stonemason Toadlet lives in grasslands and cleared areas that flood easily. The mating call is a loud "click". Males call in summer, from the edges of flooded grasslands or moist areas away from exposed water.

the FACTS!

BREEDING OCCURS in spring, summer and autumn after rain. Males often start calling before moving to marshy or flooded areas or the edges of shallow ponds to breed. The eggs are laid one at a time and attached to leaves, twigs and stems in the water. In some species, as soon as the egg is fertilised, the female dives under the water and attaches it to a stem or twig. She selects a different site for each egg until all are laid.

THE TADPOLES OF GUNGANS are bottom-dwellers that mainly feed on sediment and algae. They are usually found near the water's edge and around water plants and submerged leaf litter. The upper and lower edge of the tail fin is mottled or spotted while the rest of the fin is clear. The tadpoles take about three months to develop into little frogs and leave the water.

NORTH-WESTERN RARITIES

The Kimberley region of Western Australia and the Top End of the Northern Territory are the home to many unique and wonderful animals. This part of Australia is renowned for its spectacular escarpments, deep gorges and extensive wetlands. The region is hot and dry for much of the year but the deep gorges provide homes for plants and animals that prefer cooler and moister conditions. The rugged country acts as a barrier and a refuge, so some species that occur here have very restricted distributions indeed.

This region is important for toadlets. Seven species are restricted to particular parts of the Kimberley. These include: the Jabiru Toadlet in the Alligator Rivers area; Derby Toadlet (*Uperoleia aspera*), Derby-Broome area; Northern Toadlet (*Uperoleia borealis*), North East Kimberley area; Fat Toadlet (*Uperoleia crassa*), North West Kimberley area; Small Toadlet (*Uperoleia minima*, bottom right) Mitchell Plateau; Mole Toadlet (*Uperoleia talpa*), North Derby; Howard River Toadlet (*Uperoleia daviesae*), Howard and Elizabeth River area; and Mjoberg's Toadlet (*Uperoleia mjobergii*, top right) from the Fitzroy River area.

Anura — Myobatrachidae

Crinias
— same but different

Order: Anura
Family: Myobatrachidae

Many frogs are easy to identify because they have a distinctive appearance, while others are difficult to tell apart. The fifteen species of Crinia *froglets are all very similar, but common variations in colour and patterning can make even frogs of the same species look quite different.*

THESE SMALL FROGS GROW to 2–3 cm and they occur throughout Australia, except for the arid centre. One way researchers tell the species apart is by listening to their mating calls. All *Crinia* spp. froglets make clicking sounds but the way they call is different.

the FACTS!

THE COMMON EASTERN FROGLET (above) is found throughout the wetter parts of south-eastern Australia from the central coast of Queensland to Tasmania. It is always near water.

"SIBLING SPECIES" is the name given to species that are very closely related and difficult to separate from each other. This is in recognition of their close relationship (sibling means brother or sister). Many sibling species may have only evolved in recent times.

ANIMALS AND PLANTS that have common variations of colour and patterning in a single population are known as polymorphic (*poly* — "many", *morphe* — "form" or "many forms").

Above: From the 1950s until the 1970s, zoologists studying the Common Eastern (or Clicking) Froglet (*Crinia signifera*) found that it was not a single species at all. Studies of mating calls and genetics uncovered several very similar species.

CALLING MALE FROGLETS often react to the calls of other males and match the number of notes they are making. They may also call together at the same time.

THERE ARE HYBRIDS in some areas where the ranges of different froglets overlap. These hybrids often have calls that are intermediate between the two parent species.

HEAR NO EVIL

Froglets make a wide range of sounds described as clicking, quacking, bleating, buzzing, creaking, tinkling, squelching and chirping. While the human ear cannot tell the different froglets' calls apart, laboratory experiments have shown that female frogs can recognise the mating calls of their own species.

The differences are in the detail. Some calls may have a higher pitch, others repeat the same sound regularly, while others are uttered at different speeds or have other sounds added.

Above: It does not matter what a male Common Eastern Froglet looks like, he will still make the same mating call.

Conservation Watch
All species of froglets are considered to be Secure. Some species such as the Wallum Froglet may be locally threatened but most are common.

DIFFERENT COLOURS

It is common to find individual froglets that look more like those of other species than they do to their own brothers and sisters because froglets vary greatly in skin texture and colour.

Froglets may have smooth, ridged or warty skin while their backs may be striped, mottled or plain. Some of these forms are more common than others in particular places or in certain conditions. For example, Common Eastern Froglets with ridged backs are more numerous at high altitudes than those with ridged skin.

Right: The Sign-bearing Froglet (*Crinia insignifera*) is found along the coastal plain of South-West Western Australia; it is a variable species within its range.

Above: The Beeping Froglet occurs from southern Queensland to eastern South Australia. It is common in disturbed habitats.

LITTLE OPPORTUNISTS

Froglets, unlike many other Australian frogs, are opportunists that will breed any time when conditions are suitable.

Some, like the Beeping Froglet, (*Crinia parinsignifera*) can be heard calling all year round, although calling is more intense after rain at certain times of the year.

Froglets will breed in ponds, shallow lakes, soaks, slow-flowing streams, pools, flooded paddocks and even drains and roadside gutters.

UNUSUAL FROGLETS

Most froglets live anywhere where there is adequate moisture in natural or disturbed environments. This includes marshes, seeps and shallow bogs. Some will also breed in shallow pools in rocky outcrops.

The Wallum Froglet (*Crinia tinnula*) only occurs in the acidic paperbark swamps and coastal heathlands of coastal South-East Queensland and Northern New South Wales. Streambank Froglets (*Crinia riparia*) live near fast-flowing streams. Their eggs are laid in a mass beneath rocks at the edges of streams. The Tasmanian Froglet (*Crinia tasmaniensis*) mainly occurs in high mountain country above 600 m.

Above: Tadpoles of the Wallum Froglet are strong swimmers and dart amongst the leaf litter at the bottom of ponds.

the FACTS!

THE MOSS FROGLET (*Crinia nimbus*) is the most unusual of all. It lives in the mountain moorlands and lowland rainforests of Tasmania and differs from other froglets in the way that it breeds. The eggs are laid in small concealed nests built with clumps of moss, peat and lichen. They are large and laid in clutches of 4–16 individual eggs. After hatching, tadpoles remain in the liquid jelly until they emerge as froglets during the following spring.

SOME RESEARCHERS think that the Moss Froglet does not belong in the genus *Crinia* because its breeding behaviour is so different. If they are correct, the scientific name will be *Bryobatrachus nimbus*. The generic (first) name literally means "moss frog".

MALE CRINIA usually call from the ground in leaf litter or in grass or other plants close to water.

CROSSES BETWEEN DIFFERENT SPECIES of froglets are not always successful. The eggs may be infertile, the embryos may not develop properly or the tadpoles and young frogs may suffer from various abnormalities.

Crinias
— more of the same

Order: Anura
Family: Myobatrachidae

The majority of froglets occur in the temperate lower half of Australia, especially in wetter coastal or near coastal regions. One species occurs in parts of the dry outback, while two others are found in parts of the hot tropical north.

ONLY TWO CRINIA SPECIES inhabit the far north of Australia and one of them even occurs in southern New Guinea. Neither species occurs outside of the Tropics.

The Northern or Torrid Froglet (*Crinia remota*) was first discovered in New Guinea before it was found on Cape York Peninsula, the east coast of the Northern Territory and along the Queensland coast to the Townsville region. It lives mainly in paperbark and pandanus swamps, billabongs and flood-prone grassland.

The Top End of the Northern Territory and the Kimberly region of Western Australia is the home of the Bilingual Froglet (*Crinia bilingua*, top left). It is so-named because its call has two parts — a short grating sound and long bleat or trill.

Right: The Northern Froglet has the most northerly distribution of any froglet.

the FACTS!

WHEN A GENUS CONTAINS only one animal it is described as being "monotypic" (*mono* meaning "single" and *typus* meaning "type"). This usually occurs when an animal (or plant) is so different or highly specialised that it is hard to find their nearest relatives. Sometimes, these animals are the last survivors of their kind — or sometimes scientists and naturalists have yet to find the other species!

THE FROGLETS of the genera *Crinia*, *Geocrinia* and *Paracrinia* are all closely related and very similar in appearance. In the past, these similarities lead researchers to believe that they all belonged to a single genus, *Crinia*.

THE NORTHERN FROGLET occurs in the southern lowlands of New Guinea and may even extend into adjacent parts of West Papua, Indonesia.

LIKE OTHER CRINIA, the Northern Froglet is polymorphic. There are four common variations in pattern. The back can be light with black sides; grey to brown with dark patches; dark along the spine with bordering brown and grey stripes; or light with an incomplete band down the spine, long skin folds and black sides.

THE OUTBACK FROGLET

The Desert or Chirping Froglet (*Crinia deserticola*, below) occurs through inland parts of the Northern Territory and Queensland as well as adjacent parts of South Australia and New South Wales. It is very similar to the Beeping Froglet but has a very different mating call which sounds like the chirping of a young House Sparrow (*Passer domesticus*).

This froglet grows to 1.8 cm and inhabits damp areas such as creek beds, clay pans, soaks and river channels. It can also be found near rocky areas where there is permanent water. The males call from the ground and the eggs are laid in small clumps and attached to water plants.

Paracrinia & Geocrinias

Order: Anura
Family: Myobatrachidae

Conservation Watch
The White-bellied Frog (*Geocrinia alba*) is Endangered and the Orange-bellied Frog (*Geocrinia vitellina*) is Vulnerable.

Anura — Myobatrachidae

*Haswell's Froglet (*Paracrinia haswelli*) is one of a kind. It is the only member of the genus* Paracrinia, *although it resembles a large froglet (*Crinia *or* Geocrinia *spp.). The froglet lives in wet and dry eucalypt forests and heathlands along the east coast and adjacent tablelands of New South Wales and eastern Victoria.*

IT IS USUALLY FOUND NEAR CREEKS, swamps and dams. This frog is light grey to brown with irregular darker flecks. It has a black stripe that runs from the nostril, through the eye and down the side. Some frogs also have a pale stripe running down the spine. The belly is light brown with pale flecks. There are red patches on the backs of the thighs, the groin and at the base of each arm. It grows to 3.5 cm long.

Above: The similarity of Haswell's Froglet to other froglet species is reflected in its generic name (genus), *Paracrinia*, which can be translated as *para* meaning "like" or "above" *Crinia*.

SOUTHERN FROGLETS

The froglets of the genus *Geocrinia* are closely related to *Crinia*. They are only found in temperate southern Australia. All are small (2.5–3.5 cm) and very similar but they can be separated by distribution and call. Three species are water breeders — they lay their eggs in clumps attached to the stems of plants above the surface of the water or growing along the water's edge. When the tadpoles hatch, they fall into the water and continue life as "normal" tadpoles. The others lay their eggs in concealed depressions, shallow holes, or short tunnels in clay or mud next to water. Here the tadpoles hatch and complete their development while being nourished by their egg yolk. The tadpoles do not feed.

Left: Lea's Frog (*Geocrinia leai*) breed mainly after rains during autumn.

the FACTS!

HASWELL'S Froglet (above) is also known as the Red-groined Froglet

THE MATING CALL of Haswell's Froglet is a short, slowly repeated "ank" and can be heard after rain mainly from August to March, but all year round in warmer areas. Males call from under leaf litter or vegetation up to three metres from water or while floating in the water at the edge of pools. Eggs are laid in loose clusters of 8–80 eggs and attached to plant stems below the water's surface. Individual females have been found carrying 100 to nearly 300 eggs.

THERE ARE SEVEN SPECIES of *Geocrinia*. Most have very small distributions. The most wide-ranging are the Smooth Frog (*Geocrinia laevis*) — found in Tasmania and parts of Victoria and South Australia — and the Eastern Smooth Frog (*Geocrinia victoriana*) — found in Victoria and the south-east of New South Wales.

THE MOST COMMON SPECIES of *Geocrinia* in Western Australia is Lea's Frog (*Geocrinia leai*) which occurs throughout the South West.

Pseudophryne
— an Australian icon

Order: Anura
Family: Myobatrachidae

There can be little doubt that the brightly patterned Southern Corroboree Frog (Pseudophryne corroboree) is one of the most striking and best known Australian frogs. The small frog has eye-catching black and yellow stripes and it has appeared on everything from tourist brochures to tea towels.

THE SOUTHERN CORROBOREE FROG, and the similar Northern Corroboree Frog (*Pseudophryne pengilleyi*), inhabit the high country of the Australian Alps and the ranges to the north. The southern species favours marshlands and eucalypt forests where it may be found under logs and in vegetation.

Above: The Southern Corroboree Frog has bright golden-yellow stripes.

SOUTHERN CORROBOREE FROG

The bright golden-yellow and black stripes on the back, sides and legs of the Southern Corroboree Frog distinguish it from all other Australian frogs, except for the Northern Corroboree Frog. The skin on the back is warty or lumpy with long thick ridges. The belly is marbled black and white, or black and yellow and the frog grows to 3 cm.

The area inhabited by the Southern Corroboree Frog is not only popular with tourists, but is subject to many different land use demands, fires and climate change. Sadly, the pressures on the frog's habitat have contributed to this iconic little frog becoming Endangered and its northern relative being regarded as Vulnerable.

the FACTS!

THE NORTHERN CORROBOREE FROG (above) is very similar to its southern relative (right), but its stripes are narrower and a greener shade of yellow.

THE MATING CALL of the Southern Corroboree Frog is a short, repeated, grating "ark". The frog has a short breeding season because it lives in a cold environment. Males call during summer from concealed sites in sphagnum bogs. Mating occurs in depressions in the moss. Females lay their eggs in nests that are hollowed out near the roots of sphagnum clumps. The embryos develop inside the eggs and the tadpoles hatch when winter rains or spring snow melt flood the nest.

SOUTHERN CORROBOREE FROG EGGS are large — about 3.5 mm in diameter and laid in clutches of 10–30. The tadpoles are small and black to brown in colour. As the tadpoles approach metamorphosis the gold and black colour patterns start to appear.

Conservation Watch
The Southern Corroboree Frog is Endangered. The Northern Corroboree Frog and the Magnificent Brood Frog are Vulnerable.

A SPLASH OF RED

The other eleven species of brood frog or toadlet (*Pseudophryne* spp.) are not so flamboyantly patterned as the two corroboree frogs. However, many do sport shades of red, orange or yellow in their colour patterns. These splashes of colour range from orange, red or copper washes on the back, like the Great Brown Brood Frog (*Pseudophryne major*, right), to red "caps" and orange or yellow "epaulettes". The combinations of colours can be useful in distinguishing the different species of brood frogs.

Brood frogs lay their eggs on moist ground. The tadpoles develop within the eggs, and once they reach hatching size, will become dormant until rising water levels cover the eggs or rain carries the eggs into a suitable water body. The eggs will then hatch, releasing the tadpoles into the water.

the FACTS!

NICHOLL'S TOADLET (*Metacrinia nichollsi*), from the south-west corner of Western Australia is a close relative of the brood frog.

THE MAGNIFICENT BROOD FROG (*Pseudophryne covacevichae*, below) is a strikingly coloured frog that is only found in the vicinity of Ravenshoe, North Queensland. The breeding call is a short, squelch-like "ark" repeated at irregular intervals. Males will also give rapid chirping calls when disturbed.

Above: It does not matter what the colour pattern is on the back of a brood frog, all species have a bright black and white belly. The skin texture is coarse and rather grainy.

THE GREAT BROWN BROOD FROG (below) often has a raised dark pattern on the back that forms the shape of a lyre.

Above: The Red-crowned Toadlet (*Pseudophryne australis*) is well named.

WHAT'S IN A NAME?

The remaining eleven species of *Pseudophryne* occur throughout the south-east, and central and southern coasts of Western Australia. These little frogs range in size from 2.5–4.5 cm and are known as toadlets or brood frogs. Toadlet refers to their similarity to small true toads (family: Bufonidae), while brood frog refers to their breeding habit. Many naturalists prefer not to use the name toadlet to avoid confusion with the introduced Cane Toad (*Rhinella marina*).

Western Australian endemics

Conservation Watch
The Sunset Frog is considered to be Endangered.

Order: Anura
Family: Myobatrachidae

Western Australia is home to three very unusual frogs. All three are the sole members of their genus and are quite unlike other Australian frogs in appearance or behaviour.

THE SUNSET FROG

The Sunset Frog (*Spicospina flammocaerulea*) was only described as a new species in 1997 and is one of Australia's most spectacular frogs. Its back is black or very dark grey with bright red-orange patches on the lower half of the body, around the sides and on the hands and feet. The throat, front of the chest and undersides of the hands and feet are also bright orange. The belly has small blue spots on a blackish background. The Sunset Frog lives in isolated and permanently moist peat-based swamps. It is known from only 27 sites, all near Walpole in the extreme south-west of Western Australia. The mating call is a rapidly repeated "dd-duk-duk", which can be heard in late spring and summer from shallow water.

Right: The Sunset Frog grows to 3.5 cm and it has lots of large raised glands on its back.

the FACTS!

SANDHILL FROGS (*Arenophryne rotunda*, above and below) are squat, burrowing frogs with very short limbs. They are common on coastal sand dunes, as well as in red sand shrublands and heaths further inland and they burrow head first into the soil. Sandhill Frogs are pale brown to grey-white with fine darker flecks of green, brick red and brown. The call of these frogs is described as a short "squelch". The eggs are creamy-white and are laid at depths of 80 cm in moist sand.

NEW SPECIES OF FROGS are constantly being discovered in Australia and around the world. Some are found only because scientists have ventured into very remote places. Some are "new" because they have previously been mistaken for a similar species. Some have simply been overlooked.

ALGAL MATS at the water's surface often support the eggs of the Sunset Frog, which are laid individually.

THE TURTLE FROG

Turtle Frogs (*Myobatrachus gouldii*) have small heads, eyes, arms and legs, with a round bulbous body. They are dull grey to brown and have dirty white bellies with brown flecks. The frogs, which grow to 4.5 cm, live beneath logs in sandy soils and come to the surface after rain. They burrow head first into the sand with their arms.

Turtle Frogs feed entirely on termites and are not widespread outside the forested areas of Western Australia. The mating call is a single "ba-a-a-r-k". Male and female pairs burrow in the sand, mate and lay their eggs, which are the largest of all Australian frog eggs (5–7 mm in diameter). A female will lay 15–20 eggs at one time below ground like the Sandhill Frog. Tadpoles develop entirely within the eggs and emerge as frogs.

Ranidae
— the true frogs

Order: Anura
Family: Ranidae

Conservation Watch
The Australian Wood Frog is common and Secure.

The true frogs (Ranidae) occur almost worldwide, commonly found in Eurasia, Africa, North America and parts of South America. True frogs occur throughout the islands to Australia's north with some 50 species in New Guinea and the Solomon Islands.

A SINGLE SPECIES of true frog is found in Australia's northern Wet Tropics, Cape York Peninsula and the islands of Torres Strait, as well as in New Guinea. The Australian Wood Frog (*Sylvirana daemeli*) is a sharp-snouted, ground-dwelling to semi-aquatic frog. It grows to 8 cm and has long legs and a streamlined body. Several similar, closely-related wood frogs also inhabit New Guinea. The distribution pattern of this frog and its nearest relatives indicates that the Australian Wood Frog is a recent natural immigrant to the shores of Australia, arriving via Torres Strait.

Above: The Australian Wood Frog is a recent immigrant to our shores.

the FACTS!

THE WOOD FROG is pale to rich chocolate-brown with a few darker flecks and blotches. It has a dark stripe from the snout to the eye and dark sides. The lower arms and legs are brown with dark brown cross-bars. The belly is white and usually heavily flecked with brown. The frog has a fold of skin that runs down the back from behind the eye. Finger and toe pads are small.

THE MATING CALL of the Wood Frog is a series of low quacks. Males call throughout spring, summer and autumn. The frogs lay thousands of eggs in large masses in still or slow-flowing water. The tadpoles can grow up to 6 cm long and are black and gold.

THE VOCAL SACS of Australian male frogs usually expand like little balloons under the throat. The Australian Wood Frog is an exception; it has a vocal sac that expands as two lobes on either side of the head.

VORACIOUS PREDATORS

Wood frogs are voracious predators and will readily catch any small animals they can overpower. They have acute vision and will respond to any sign of movement. If such movement reveals a potential threat, they will not hesitate to leap into water for safety.

Australian Wood Frogs live in a variety of habitats, including rainforests, dry monsoon forests and tropical woodlands. They are often seen at night near or around the edges of lagoons and along the banks of streams.

Anura — Microhylidae

Microhylids
— narrow-mouthed frogs

Order: Anura
Family: Microhylidae

Australasian narrow-mouthed frogs are tropical rainforest frogs that range from the southern Philippines, through eastern Indonesia, to New Guinea and tropical northern Australia. There are 219 species and 19 of these occur in the rainforests and monsoon forests of northern Australia.

AUSTRALIAN MICROHYLIDS include the fourteen species of nursery-frogs (*Cophixalus,* spp.) and the five species of Whistle Frogs (*Austrochaperina,* spp.). Most are small (1.5–2.5 cm), but the two largest species, the Black Mountain Boulderfrog (*Cophixalus saxatilis*) and Cape Melville Boulderfrog (*Cophixalus zweifeli*), grow to 4 cm.

the FACTS!

THE ORNATE NURSERY-FROG lays around 10–20 large eggs in strings on the ground. The male has been observed guarding the eggs. Tadpoles spend their entire time in the egg capsules and feed off the yolk. They hatch fully developed.

SEVERAL OTHER SPECIES of nursery-frogs are found in Tropical North Queensland, including two species of "boulder" frogs. The Black Mountain Boulderfrog (above) is found only at Black Mountain near Cooktown, while the Cape Melville Boulderfrog is restricted to suitable habitat in the Cape Melville National Park. Most nursery-frogs, like the Mountain-top Nursery-frog (*Cophixalus monticola*, top) are found only at high elevations in the Wet Tropics. Mating calls include high pitched trills, clicks, buzzes and rattling sounds. Males of the Elegant Frog (*Cophixalus concinnus*) have a red, black and white throat, which is easily seen when they call.

Above: The Tapping Nursery-frog (*Cophixalus aenigma*) occurs at elevations above 750 m in the ranges north of Cairns.

ORNATE NURSERY-FROG

The Ornate Nursery-frog (*Cophixalus ornatus*) is one of the more common microhylids. A rainforest inhabitant, it is usually found under leaf litter or concealed among plants during the day. The Ornate Nursery-frog grows to about 2.5 cm and is grey to sandy-brown. It has a yellow and black bar between the eyes and a W-shaped mark over shoulders. There are numerous warts and skin-folds on the back.

Left: The mating call of the Ornate Nursery-frog is a short beep.

Conservation Watch

Although several microhylids have very small distributions, none are under threat. There are concerns about the impact of climate change on some of the more restricted mountain top species, such as the Elegant Frog.

Anura — Microhylidae

FOREST FLOOR WHISTLERS

The Rain Frog (*Austrochaperina pluvialis*) and Fry's Frog (*Austrochaperina fryi*) are found throughout the rainforests of the Wet Tropics. The Robust Whistle-frog (*Austrochaperina robusta*) occurs in high altitude rainforest in the same area, while the Slender Frog (*Austrochaperina gracilipes*) inhabits rainforests, monsoon forests, sandstone outcrops and paperbark swamps on northern Cape York Peninsula.

Below: The Rain Frog is also known as the White-browed Whistle-frog, for the distinctive streaks over its eyes and snout.

the FACTS!

THE NORTHERN TERRITORY WHISTLE-FROG (*Austrochaperina adelphe*) is the only microhylid that is found outside Queensland. It lives in permanent swamps, streams, savannah woodlands, monsoon forest and melaleuca swamps in the far north of the Northern Territory. This frog is found under leaf litter and near soaks.

Below: The Slender Frog

THE WHISTLE-FROGS

Whistle-frogs (*Austrochaperina* spp.) are robust little frogs (2–3 cm) that live in the leaf litter, rock piles and logs on the rainforest floor. Males all make high-pitched cheeping, chirping or peeping calls. Like the nursery-frogs, the eggs are laid on the ground in damp conditions and concealed under rocks, logs or other debris. Egg clutches range from 9–12 in number and are attended or straddled by an adult, usually the male. All development occurs in the egg and the young hatch as miniature adults.

Left: Fry's Frog from the Wet Tropics.

Anura — Bufonidae

Cane Toad
— ecological catastrophe

Order: Anura
Family: Bufonidae

The Cane Toad (Rhinella marina, *formerly* Bufo marinus), *also known as the Giant American or Marine Toad, is native to Central and South America, but has the widest range of any "true" toad in the world. It is one of Australia's worst environmental pests — thanks to humans.*

IN 1935, SOME 3400 young cane toads were released around Cairns, Gordonvale and Innisfail in Tropical North Queensland in the hope that they would control two serious insect pests, the Grey-back (*Dermolepida albohirtum*) and Frenchi Beetles (*Lepidiota frenchi*). The toads proved to be useless as biological control agents, but highly successful as environmental pests and general nuisances.

the FACTS!

ATTEMPTS WERE MADE to introduce foreign animals to control pests in sugar cane plantations during the early 20th century. These included the Common Myna, which have been described as the "Cane Toads of the air".

MALE CANE TOADS are known to engage in a breeding frenzy (above), at such times they will try and mate with anything that moves. Females that get caught up in these frenzies can be injured.

CANE TOADS have been introduced to the Caribbean Islands, southern United States, Hawaii, New Guinea and several Pacific islands. In every place they have become highly invasive pests.

JUVENILE CANE TOADS (below) often have small orange or brick-red spots scattered over their back.

A HARDY OPPORTUNIST

Toads are still actively spreading across northern and eastern Australia. Cane Toads favour disturbed areas such as farms, parks and gardens as well as clearings, along roads and tracks in forested areas. They do occur in more natural areas but are rarely encountered in extensive rainforest or at higher elevations. It is hardly surprising that the Cane Toad has become a pest because it is one of Nature's supreme opportunists. It breeds prolifically in all but the coldest weather and is a very hardy animal with no special habitat requirements to survive.

The Cane Toad has leathery, warty skin, thick bony ridges on the snout and sides of the face, distinct "eyelids" and conspicuous enlarged poison glands above and behind exposed ear discs (parotoid glands). Female toads grow to 12 cm and some rare specimens can reach 25 cm; males are smaller reaching 11 cm.

Conservation Watch
The Cane Toad is an introduced invasive, environmental pest.

Anura — Bufonidae

AN INSATIABLE APPETITE

Like all large frogs, Cane Toads will eat anything they can catch. This includes small mammals, lizards and other frogs, but mostly they eat ground-dwelling insects such as ants, termites and beetles. The toads will also steal food left out for cats and dogs. Perhaps the only limiting factor to the size of the cane toad's prey is the size of its mouth!

Despite, their taste for beetles, the toads failed to control cane beetles because these insects are rarely found on the ground where cane toads live. Added to this, the Cane Toad's wide-ranging diet meant that it did not depend on cane beetles for food.

It has been estimated that a female Cane Toad can lay up to 40,000 eggs in a single breeding season.

TOXIC TOAD

Cane Toads possess skin glands that produce a thick, milky secretion when the animal is under threat. This secretion is a cocktail of toxins that prove deadly to other animals. Most of the toxins are secreted by the swollen neck (parotoid glands), with lesser amounts from the skin on the back. It is not uncommon for family pets and native predators to die after they have ingested toad toxins. In the wild, toads compete for food, shelter and breeding sites with native animals. Toads are toxic at all stages of their life.

Below: A large female Cane Toad, note the huge poison glands.

the FACTS!

THE NORTHERN TERRITORY GOVERNMENT is considering a number of different methods to halt the march of the Cane Toad across Australia's Top End. This includes trapping (below) and the erection of barrier fences.

IT IS OFTEN CLAIMED that Cane Toads can "spit" their poisonous secretions but this is not correct. These reports usually come from people who have ruptured a toad's poison glands or splashed secretions from its back while striking it. Cane Toads will eject a stream of urine when disturbed, but this is harmless. It is possible that the pores that connect the poison gland to the surface of the toad have been plugged by tissue and may "pop like a wine cork" under pressure.

IT IS AN INCORRECT MYTH that a dead, dry toad is harmless. This is not so; the poisonous secretions are not neutralised by drying or freezing and will reconstitute on contact with the moist membranes of the mouth and upper respiratory system.

Threats to frogs
— an uncertain future

Amphibians have lived on the Earth for hundreds of millions of years. Most early amphibians became extinct around 250 million years ago during the Permian Mass Extinction. Now in the 21st century, the world's amphibians could be facing another mass extinction.

FROGS FACE MANY THREATS to their survival. Some pressures occur in particular places and only affect a small number of species. Others affect many species over very wide areas. Many human activities can cause frog populations to decline. It is important to recognise how our actions impact on our environment.

Above: Protection of natural habitats and wetlands, like this paperbark swamp, will shield frogs and other wildlife from many but not all threats.

THREATENING PROCESSES

The things that cause species to become endangered or extinct are known as threatening processes. These include habitat loss, introduced species, environmental pollution, disease and climate change. These things may affect animals in many different places at the same time.

A frog's habitat is the environment where it feeds, shelters and breeds. Habitat loss and degradation is the greatest threat facing amphibians today and it has the potential to affect almost 4000 species worldwide. The number of species impacted by habitat loss and degradation is almost four times greater than the next most common threat, which is pollution.

Left: Heavy metals and other forms of pollution cause abnormalities, such as the growth of multiple legs, in frogs.

the FACTS!

HABITAT LOSS clearly poses the greatest threat to amphibians, but a newly recognised fungal disease is seriously affecting an increasing number of species across the globe. Perhaps most disturbing, many amphibian populations are declining for unknown reasons, complicating efforts to save these precious animals.

DISEASE EPIDEMICS can cause sudden, dramatic population declines in affected species. Although habitat loss affects many more plants and animals, disease can strike unexpectedly even in undisturbed habitats.

FIRE AND FREQUENT BURNING may kill frogs and change their habitat. As human populations expand and the growth of towns and cities destroys patches of bush where frogs shelter, it prevents them moving from one area to another.

FROGS, THEIR EGGS and tadpoles are vulnerable to many of the things that reduce water quality. Contamination by pesticides, detergents, fertilisers, chemicals and heavy metals all threaten frogs. Frogs are placed at risk by increased salinity (most frogs are salt intolerant), toxic algal blooms and low oxygen levels in water.

Conservation Watch

Many frog species are threatened by habitat destruction, pollution, disease and climate change.

THINK GREEN

Humans can damage frog habitat in many ways. For example, people may clear large areas of native vegetation for housing and agriculture, drain wetlands, or allow cattle and sheep to graze and trample on wetlands. Introduced weeds may also make an area unsuitable for frogs by choking streams and wetlands. Even seemingly-harmless activities such as collecting bush rocks removes shelter sites for ground-dwelling frogs.

Left: Watercourses are vulnerable to invasive weeds, damage by feral animals and human traffic. If water or habitat conditions change, so will the frog species using the streams.

CLIMATE CHANGE

Expanding human populations are changing the nature of the planet. As a result of human activities, levels of carbon dioxide in the Earth's atmosphere are rising and contributing to a rise in temperatures worldwide. This phenomenon, known as "global warming", is placing many species at risk, but at the same time is responsible for forcing some tropical species to move into temperate regions.

Right: Industrial emissions have been identified as a major contributor to climate change.

TAKING STOCK

Nearly one-third (about 1896 species) of the world's amphibian species are threatened; more than any other type of animal. At least 34 amphibian species are known to be extinct, while another 130 species have not been found in recent years and may be extinct. At least 43% of all amphibian populations are declining so the number of threatened species will rise in future. In contrast, fewer than 1% of species show population increases.

Left: Common household chemicals are toxic to frogs and can create harm if they end up in waterways and wetlands.

the FACTS!

THE LARGEST NUMBERS of threatened amphibians occur in Latin American countries such as Colombia (approx. 209), Mexico (approx. 198), and Ecuador (approx. 163). The highest levels of threat, however, are in the Caribbean. More than 80% of amphibians are threatened in the Dominican Republic, Cuba, and Jamaica, and a staggering 92% in Haiti.

ENVIRONMENTAL POLLUTION is especially threatening to frogs, because pollutants are easily absorbed through the soft skin of adult animals and through the gills of tadpoles. Because frogs live on land and in water, they may have more opportunities to be exposed to environmental contaminants than other animals.

NOT ALL NATIVE FROGS are threatened by environmental change, which affects species and communities differently. The Striped Marsh-frog (below) is thriving.

MORE THAN 40,000 industrial chemicals are registered for use in Australia in addition to more than 4500 agricultural and 3000 veterinary products. The impact of many of these products on frog populations is unknown.

Frog declines
— a worldwide threat

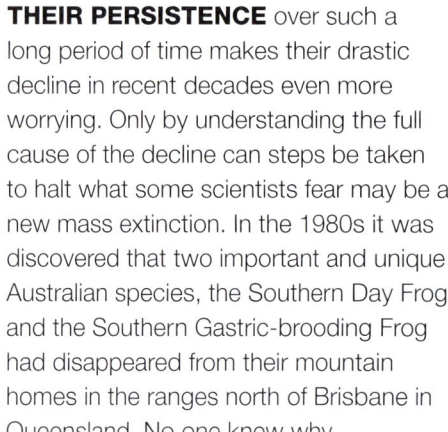

Australia is home to nearly 220 species of frogs, with new species being discovered all the time. It is a significant centre of amphibian diversity. Frogs have existed in Australia for approximately 45 million years, surviving a wide range of climatic changes and other environmental disturbances.

THEIR PERSISTENCE over such a long period of time makes their drastic decline in recent decades even more worrying. Only by understanding the full cause of the decline can steps be taken to halt what some scientists fear may be a new mass extinction. In the 1980s it was discovered that two important and unique Australian species, the Southern Day Frog and the Southern Gastric-brooding Frog had disappeared from their mountain homes in the ranges north of Brisbane in Queensland. No one knew why.

GLOBAL CONCERNS

Similar reports of declining and "missing" frogs started appearing from other parts of the world at about the same time. Of particular concern is the disappearance of frogs not only from disturbed sites, but also from pristine habitats away from human interference.

Twenty-seven Australian frog species (13%) are now classed as Threatened, and of these, eight species may have disappeared altogether. An additional fourteen species are declining. The reasons for this are still being investigated and scientists are finding out more every day about how different activities can combine to impact on frog survival.

The loss of some frog species can be put down to specific human actions in certain areas, but this does not explain all declines and extinctions of frogs.

Above: The future for the Southern Corroboree Frog is uncertain because it faces multiple threats to its habitat.

Above: Some stream-dwelling mountain frogs, like the Common Mistfrog, have proved to be very vulnerable to disease epidemics.

Above: It is hard to predict the future for some frogs, such as the Green-thighed Frog, because they are very difficult to study and unpredictable in their behaviour.

the FACTS!

THE GLOBAL NATURE of world frog declines first came to light during the First World Congress of Herpetology in 1989.

APPEARANCE OF CHYTRID FUNGUS in a frog population is likely to make those frogs less able to cope with other threats, say some scientists. The death of adult frogs from the disease as well as predation by introduced fish, habitat fragmentation and pollution may all increase the likelihood of extinction.

FROGS FROM HIGH ALTITUDES, like the Southern Day Frog (above), are very susceptible to chytrid fungus infection. Experiments have shown that infected frogs are more likely to die at low temperatures. In addition, stream-dwellers are vulnerable to the fungus being carried in water.

SOME SPECIAL FROGS, like the Cooloola Sedgefrog (below) and the Wallum Sedgefrog (top right on page 73) are reasonably secure because a sizeable part of their range is contained in national parks and other reserves.

Conservation Watch
Long-snouted Frog from Cape York Peninsula (far left) is Secure. Waterfall Frog (left) from Queensland's Wet Tropics is Endangered.

CHYTRID FUNGUS

Chytridiomycosis (pronounced ky-trid-ee-o-my-co-sis) is caused by a type of fungus, *Batrachochytrium dendrobatidis*, and it is a highly infectious frog killer. In some frog populations the disease has caused only a few random deaths, but in others 100% of animals have died. The disease was identified in Australia in 1998, but has since been recorded in New Zealand, Europe, North America, Central America, South America and Africa. Using museum specimens, scientists have been able to show that Chytridiomycosis has been affecting amphibians worldwide since at least 1978.

Chytrid fungus attacks the parts of a frog's skin that contain keratin, a tough, fibrous substance that forms hair, nails and horns etc. The skin of a sick frog gets thicker and sometimes looks different. The fungus is thought to release toxins that are absorbed directly through the frog's skin, damaging the skin so badly that the frog's water balance and breathing are affected. It also damages the nervous system, affecting the frog's behaviour.

Left: Declines of the Southern Green and Golden Bell Frog have mainly affected highland populations.

the FACTS!

TADPOLES CAN ALSO CARRY the chytrid fungus, but since they do not have keratin in their mouths, they are not affected until they start to turn into frogs. Sometimes the fungus can have a localised effect on the tadpole's mouth parts, causing them to fall out or be damaged.

THE CHYTRID DISEASE may not kill frogs immediately, thus they can move to other areas before they die, spreading fungal spores to new ponds and streams.

THE GREEN AND GOLDEN BELL FROG (below) faces many threats. Its eggs and tadpoles are known to be destroyed by introduced mosquitofish (*Gambusia* spp.).

EASILY SPREAD

The chytrid fungus was probably introduced to Australia through the trade in exotic pets, such as axolotls or possibly through aquarium fish.

It can be spread by:
- the movement of infected frogs in agricultural produce ("banana box" frogs);
- wet soil on the shoes of bushwalkers;
- flooding;
- water birds;
- motor vehicle tyres in the wet weather;
- releasing frogs and tadpoles somewhere different from where they were found; and
- moving pond plants from infected water.

Right, top and bottom: Chytrid disease can affect almost any frog large or small irrespective of habits and ecology.

Frog enthusiasts

Frog watching
— a sensory experience

the FACTS!

MOST FROG-WATCHING GROUPS do not encourage the long term keeping of native frogs. People who wish to keep captive specimens must do so according to law and ensure the highest possible standard of care is provided. They must also respect the dignity of frogs as wild animals.

ALTHOUGH CANE TOADS are an undesirable introduction, they are also a frog in their own right and should never be treated cruelly.

THERE ARE ONLY A SMALL NUMBER of scientists undertaking research into Australian frogs, so they can't be in all places at all times. Amateur naturalists and frog-watchers can make important contributions to our knowledge of frogs by simply recording and reporting their own observations.

BE AWARE that restrictions are likely to exist on access and movement in areas where threatened frog species live. Such restrictions are necessary to contain disease threats.

Australians have become very conscious of frogs because so many species have been affected by declines. The ever-spreading Cane Toad has probably helped too — simply because people want to prevent it establishing in new parts of Australia.

WHATEVER THE REASON, frog-watching has become a popular pastime. A dedicated frog-watcher must be prepared to visit many different places if they wish to see more than just those species that live in or visit backyards.

The best time to watch frogs is at night, starting about 30 minutes after sunset. The best time for finding frogs are usually still nights after a good rain during the breeding season. The worst times are during the full moon or when it is windy; frogs are easily disturbed during bright moonlight and tend to hide when it is windy.

Above: The obvious place to look for frogs is near water. During the day, tadpoles can be observed and adults found in their retreats.

TOOLS FOR FROG SPOTTING

Frog-watching should start just after sunset, so a waterproof torch or headlamp is an essential tool. A frog-watcher will also need a watch, a thermometer, notebook and pencil. Cameras (waterproof if possible) are useful for verifying identifications and recording colour and behaviour.

Portable sound recording devices are handy for locating individual frogs. If frog calls are recorded and then played back to the same frogs, they will usually respond. By repeating the process, it is possible to track down individual frogs. Recordings of frog choruses also make useful records of when and what species occur at a given site.

For best results, use a hand-held microphone to get as close as possible to the caller. The best distance for recording varies. In general, frogs that make high-pitched sounds are likely to cause distorted recordings if the microphone is placed too close.

CODE OF ETHICS

Most frog societies around Australia try to follow general guidelines that ensure the safety of both frog-watchers and frogs. People planning to go "frogging" should follow these rules:

- take safety seriously;
- choose and use your observation area carefully;
- respect ownership;
- consider other users of the area;
- leave the area as you found it;
- avoid disturbing frogs, other animals and plants;
- do not handle frogs unnecessarily;
- safeguard rare species;
- take photographs and not specimens;
- be patient;
- report unusual events;
- give no-one cause to regret your field study; and
- scrape, scrub and disinfect to avoid spreading disease.

Above: Frog-watchers must be conscious of their impact on frogs, especially threatened species like this Waterfall Frog. Avoid handling frogs or moving about in breeding choruses.

DON'T SPREAD DISEASE!

"Froggers" must be careful not to spread chytrid disease by staying squeaky clean. All equipment used in wading, capturing, handling or transporting frogs must be scrubbed clean of debris or caked mud. It must also be doused thoroughly with household bleach. This is especially important when moving significant distances between frog sites, or when moving from one stream channel to another.

Remember: Scrape, scrub and disinfect!

Right: Dainty Green Tree-frog in full song.

LOOK, DON'T TOUCH

Native frogs, their eggs and tadpoles are protected in all States of Australia. Many of the areas they inhabit are in national parks, state forests and other reserves so access permits may be needed.

It is important that frog-watchers do not handle the animals unnecessarily, or disturb frogs when they are attempting to breed. Handling frogs may cause distress or injury and contact with dry human skin can cause irritation and stress. Keep hands moist. Watching frogs is more rewarding than handling them.

HELPFUL HINTS

- A successful frog-watcher needs to be quiet and patient — noisy clothes and equipment will alert the frogs and make them hide.
- Frogs are located by listening. Many frog-watchers cup their hands behind their ears to make it easier to hear frog calls and identify the direction they are coming from.
- Tracking frogs down is made easier if at least three people are involved. To pinpoint a frog's location, participants surround the frog, keeping roughly equal positions from each other. Each person approaches, carefully and slowly, pointing to where they think the frog will be found. This technique is called triangulation.

Frog ponds
— backyard biodiversity

Many frog populations are declining as their habitats are destroyed by human activities. However, people can create and protect suitable habitats that may benefit both common and threatened frog species.

the FACTS!

EACH FROG SPECIES has specific requirements for all types of things, like water, temperature, humidity and even barometric pressure. Some have interesting habits like burrowing underground or breeding only in running water. Make sure you research local frog species thoroughly to determine their needs.

PEOPLE HAVE SOMETIMES TRIED to introduce species into areas where they do not normally occur — mountain species into lowland areas or tropical species into temperate regions. In most cases the introduced frogs or tadpoles have simply died, but these same people may have also contributed to the spread of the chytrid fungus.

BUSHY AND LEAFY PLANTS of various heights ranging from ground cover types to trees and shrubs will attract different types of frogs. Mulch and compost will attract insects for food and provide cover for ground-dwellers.

VEGETABLE GARDENS and greenhouses are favourite places for backyard frogs because they are moist, humid and attract insects.

A CIRCULATING PUMP in a garden pond will make the water less appealing to mosquitoes.

FROG-FRIENDLY PARKS, GARDENS AND BACKYARDS provide pathways for frogs to move across the urban landscape. Frogs need lots of plant cover (especially natives), shelter sites (rocks, logs and leaf litter) and most importantly, sources of water and moisture.

It is best not to move frogs or tadpoles around, even within suburbs or over short distances of a couple of kilometres. In addition to possibly spreading chytrid disease, the new area may not be quite right for them. Newcomers may die, or they may leave to find suitable conditions. If they remain, they may interfere with frogs that belong naturally to the area.

Above: The species that can be attracted to backyards will differ across Australia. Providing leaf litter and floating vegetation will help attract frogs to your backyard.

A GARDEN IS BEST

The best and most effective way to attract frogs is to create a suitable habitat and let the frogs find it themselves! Often this approach may result in more species taking up residence in the backyard than can ever be achieved by trying to forcibly introduce frogs.

Frogs need insects to eat, places to hide and somewhere to breed. A garden that has a lot of variety will be more attractive to a wide number of species.

Left: A successful frog garden will take time to construct. The ultimate expression of success will be the natural breeding of one or more local species of frogs.

Conservation Watch

Frog ponds can make for attractive gardens and can also be refuge for frogs in an otherwise hostile urban environment.

Frog enthusiasts

BUILD A FROG POND

A frog friendly garden should have a pond. Frog ponds should be part sunny, part shady, but not placed directly under trees (to avoid toxic leaves and too much organic matter falling into the pond).

The pond should be placed in a low point where water naturally collects — such a spot may already be familiar to local frogs. Tadpoles prefer shallow water with a large surface area, so a deep, steep-sided goldfish pond is unsuitable for most frogs.

Before constructing a pond, check if there are any regulations in your area about building frog ponds and make sure young children do not have access to the pond.

Above: The majority of native frogs breed in shallow water with lots of surrounding vegetation for protection. Males will always be obvious because they call, females are secretive and not easily seen.

DON'T FORGET…

The pond should have shallow edges, a flat base and be at least 50 cm deep in one spot. It should have rocks, logs and plants in and around the pond edges, plants and logs in the pond and a base covered with washed sand or gravel.

The water must be chlorine and chemical free. If the pond is being filled with tap water, stand it in sunlight for five days, so the chlorine can dissipate. Don't use chlorine neutralising drops. Keep spare chlorine-free water on hand.

Below: Male frogs of different species call from different places around a body of water — this is how they reduce competition. If the edge of the pond is varied, it should prove attractive to more species.

the FACTS!

FROG FRIENDLY GARDENS are easy to build and maintain, but the good work can be easily undone by careless use of fertilisers, sprays and other garden and household chemicals. Frogs absorb chemicals through their skins easily or they may eat poisoned insects. Fortunately, many people are finding new ways of gardening which are not only safer for frogs, but for the gardeners themselves.

FEED TADPOLES the unwanted outer dark green leaves of a lettuce. The lettuce should be washed thoroughly to remove pesticide residues and then boiled until soft (15–20 minutes). Boiled leaves may be conveniently stored in plastic ice cube trays and frozen ready for use. Feed tadpoles as much food as they will eat every 1–3 days and remove any remaining food before re-feeding. Too much food will foul the water; not enough may result in the tadpoles eating each other.

MOSQUITO FISH (*Gambusia* spp.) should never be placed in frog ponds because they attack and eat frog eggs as well as tadpoles. Some aquarium fish may seem suitable, like the White Cloud Minnow (*Tanichthys albonubes*), but pose a risk to native fish if they ever "escape" into waterways.

77

Web links & further reading

WEBSITES:

Australian Frogs
www.frogsaustralia.net.au
www.frogs.org.au

Worldwide species
www.research.amnh.org/herpetology/amphibia
www.pbif.org/taxonomy/frogs.html

Photographs
http://calphotos.berkeley.edu/fauna

Frogwatch
www.globalamphibians.org
www.frogwatch.org.au
http://frogs.org.au/frogwatch
www.frogwatch.com.au

AUSTRALIAN MUSEUMS:

Australian Museum
www.austmus.gov.au

Qld — www.qm.qld.gov.au

WA — www.museum.wa.gov.au

SA — www.samuseum.sa.gov.au

Vic — http://museumvictoria.com.au

Tas — www.tmag.tas.gov.au

NT — www.nt.gov.au/nreta/museums/index.html

REGIONAL GUIDES:

New South Wales
www.nationalparks.nsw.gov.au
www.fats.org.au

Australian Capital Territory
www.environment.act.gov.au

Queensland
www.epa.qld.gov.au
www.qldfrogs.asn.au

Victoria
http://home.vicnet.net.au/~kes

South Australia
www.epa.sa.gov.au

Western Australia
www.museum.wa.gov.au/frogwatch

Northern Territory
www.ourterritory.com/frogs

National
www.deh.gov.au/education
www.greeningaustralia.org.au

PUBLICATIONS:

Anstis, M. *Tadpoles of South-eastern Australia: A Guide with Keys*, Reed New Holland, Frenchs Forest, NSW, Australia, 2001

Barker, J., Grigg, G.C. and Tyler, M.J. *A Field Guide To Australian Frogs*, Surrey Beatty & Sons, Sydney, Australia, 1995

Casey, K. *Attracting Frogs to Your Garden*, Kimberley Publications, Brisbane, Australia, 1996

Clyne, D. *Australian Frogs*, Lansdowne Press, Melbourne, Australia, 1969

Cogger, H.G. *Reptiles and Amphibians Of Australia*, Reed Books, Sydney, Australia 1992

Frith, C. and Frith D. *Australian Tropical Reptiles and Frogs*, Frith and Frith Books, Prionodura, 1987

Hofrichter, R. (Ed). *The Encyclopaedia of Amphibians*, Toronto, Key Porter Books, 2000

Menzies, J. *The Frogs of New Guinea and Solomon Islands*, Pensoft Publications, Sofia, 2006

Robinson, M. *A Field Guide To Frogs Of Australia*, Aust. Museum & Reed Books, Sydney, Australia, 1995

Ryan, M. J. (Ed). *Anuran Communication*, Smithsonian Institution Press, Washington, 2001

Schmida, G. *The Cold-blooded Australians*, Doubleday, Sydney, 1985

Semlitsch, R. *Amphibian conservation*, Smithsonian Institution Press, Washington DC, 2003

Stebbins, R. C. & Cohen, N.W. *A Natural History of Amphibians*, Princeton University Press, Princeton, 1995

Swan, G. *Green Guide to Frogs of Australia*, New Holland, Sydney, 2001

Tyler, M.J. *Australian Frogs, A Natural History*, Reed Books, Sydney, 1994

FIELD GUIDES:

Australian Capital Territory
Bennett, R. *Reptiles and Frogs of the Australian Capital Territory*, National Parks Association of the ACT, Woden, 1997

New South Wales
Griffiths, K. *Frogs and Reptiles of the Sydney Region*, University of NSW Press, Kensington, 1997

Northern Territory
Tyler, M.J. & Davies, M. *Frogs of the Northern Territory*, Batchelor Institute, Batchelor, N.T., 1986

Queensland
Hero, J-M. and Fickling, S. *A Guide to Stream-dwelling Frogs of the Wet Tropics Rainforests*, James Cook University Press, Townsville, 1994

Meyer, E., Hines, H.B. and Hero, J-M. *Wet Forest Frogs of South-east Queensland*, Griffith University, 2001

Ryan, M. (Ed). *Wildlife of Tropical North Queensland*, Queensland Museum, South Brisbane, 2000

Ryan, M. (Ed). *Wildlife of Greater Brisbane. (Queensland Museum*, South Brisbane, 2007

South Australia
Tyler, M.J. *The Frogs of South Australia*. South Australian Museum, Adelaide, 1977

Waite, E.R. *The Reptiles and Amphibians of South Australia,* SSAR Publications, 1994

Tasmania
Martin, A.A. and Littlejohn, M.J. *Tasmanian Amphibians*, University of Tasmania, Hobart, 1982

Littlejohn, M. *Frogs of Tasmania*, Hobart, University of Tasmania, 2003

Victoria
Hero, J-M., Littlejohn, M.J. and Marantelli, G. *Frogwatch Field Guide to Victorian Frogs*, Victorian Department of Conservation and Environment, Melbourne 1991

Museum Victoria. *Melbourne's wildlife: a field guide to the fauna of Greater Melbourne*, CSIRO Publishing and Museum Victoria, Melbourne, 2006

Western Australia
Bush, B., Maryan, B., Browne-Cooper, R. and Robinson, D. *Reptiles and Frogs of the Perth Region,* University of Western Australia Press, Perth, 1995

Dell, J. and Turpin, M. *Frogs of the Perth Area*, Western Australian Museum, Perth, 1992

Orange, P. et al. *Guide to the Wildlife of the Perth Region*, Simon Nevill Publications, Perth, 2005

Tyler, M.J., Smith, L.A. and Johnstone, R.E. *Frogs of Western Australia*, Western Australian Museum, Perth, 2000

Glossary

ALLUVIAL Usually relating to a mine, digging up of soil.

AMPHIBIAN A four-limbed, cold-blooded animal that lives both on land and in water over its life cycle.

AMPLEXUS Amphibian mating embrace; male grasps female around her groin or armpits with his front legs.

ANATOMY The structure of an animal or plant.

ANCESTOR A relative from many hundreds of years ago.

CAMOUFLAGE Colouring that helps an animal blend in to its background.

CANNIBAL An animal that eats others of its own species.

COELOM The body cavity, as distinguished from the intestinal cavity.

DIURNAL Active by day.

DORMANT In a state of rest or inactivity.

ENDEMIC Found in a particular location and nowhere else.

EVOLVE To change through descending generations.

EXTINCT Having no living examples of the same kind, or species.

FLANGE A protective ridge, for strengthening.

FOSSIL Remains or traces of a once-living organism.

GELATINOUS Jelly-like.

GENUS (PLURAL: GENERA) A group of one or more closely related species of animals/plants. The first Latin name of an animal's/plant's scientific name is the genus. Different species can share the same genus.

HABITAT Where an animal lives.

HYBRID The offspring of two animals or plants of different breeds, varieties, species, or genera.

INVERTEBRATE An animal that does not have a backbone.

LABYRINTHODONTS The first amphibians that lived more than 300 million years ago.

LARVA (PLURAL: LARVAE) Any immature animal e.g. tadpoles.

MAMMAL A class of vertebrates whose young feed upon milk from the mother's breast.

MARSUPIAL Animals that carry their young in a pouch.

MEMBRANE A thin, pliable sheet or layer of animal tissue, serving to line an organ.

METAMORPHOSIS Dramatic or total transformation from one stage in an animal's life to another, e.g. tadpole to frog.

MONTANE FOREST Forest that grows on mountains above altitude of 1000 m.

MUCOUS Slimy substance secreted by some animals.

NOCTURNAL Active at night.

PIGMENT Colouring substance. In animals, pigment is usually black, brown, yellow, red or white.

POLYMORPHIC Animals and plants that have many forms of colouring and patterning within a single population.

PREDATOR An animal that hunts and eats other animals.

REPTILES Cold-blooded vertebrates, including lizards, snakes, turtles, crocodiles, alligators.

SALAMANDER Tailed amphibians, most of which have an aquatic larval stage but are terrestrial as adults.

SLOUGHED SKIN Outer skin which has been shed.

SPAWN Eggs and sperm of frogs, fish and aquatic invertebrates.

SPECIES Group of animals that can breed together and produce fertile offspring.

TAXONOMY Scientific classification, e.g. of animals and plants.

TOXIC Poisonous.

TRIANGULATION The process "froggers" (frog-watchers) use to find a frog.

"TRUE" FROG The use of "true" is the legacy of modern scientific method and herpetology originating in Europe-North America. Ranids and bufonids are the common groups of frogs in these regions and the first to be scientifically known and studied. Everything else has therefore been an addition to the scientific knowledge base. If herpetology originated somewhere else — then a different group of frogs would be called "true" frogs. It has absolutely nothing to do with the qualities of the frogs themselves.

TUBERCLES Small conical bumps.

TYMPANUM Membranous eardrum, visible in some frogs and lizards.

UROSTYLE A bone formed by the fusion of all or part of the caudal (tail) vertebrae in frogs, toads and some fish.

VERTEBRAE Bones which make up the backbone, or vertebral column.

VERTEBRATE Animal with a backbone surrounding the spinal cord and a skull protecting the brain.

VORACIOUS Greedy in eating.

Index

A
Acid Frogs 11, 27
Adelotus brevis 38
Ambystoma mexicanum 7, 14
Arenophryne rotunda 64
Armoured Frog 28
Assa
    darlingtoni 10, 52
Australian Wood Frog 13, 65
Australobatrachus ilius 15
Austrochaperina 66–67
    adelphe 67
    fryi 67
    gracilipes 67
    pluvialis 67
    robusta 67
Axolotl 7, 14

B
Banjo Frog 44–45
    Eastern 44, 45
    Giant 44, 45
    Northern. See Scarlet-sided Pobblebonk
    Western 44
Barbourula busuangensis 53
Barking Frog 42, 43
Barred Frog 54–55
    Fleay's 10, 55
    Giant 13, 55
    Great 54, 55
    New Guinea 54
    Northern 54, 55
        tadpoles 54
    Southern. See Stuttering Frog
    tadpoles 54
    Wet Tropics 55
Baw Baw Frog 40, 41
Bell Frog 32–33
    Green and Golden 32, 33
    Southern 33
    Southern Green and Golden 73
    Western Green and Golden 33
Boulderfrog 66–67
    Black Mountain 10, 66
Bridled Frog 31
Broad-palmed Frog 30
Brood Frog 63
    Great Brown 63
    Magnificent 63
Bufo marinus 5, 13, 68
Bufonidae (family) 68–69
Bullfrog 44, 45, 48. See also Banjo Frog, Eastern
    Giant. See Banjo Frog, Giant
    Goldfields 48
    Northern. See Scarlet-sided Pobblebonk
Burrowing Frog 2, 11, 46
    Giant 46–47
    Northern 48
    Ornate 46
    Spencer's 11, 46, 47
        tadpoles 47

C
Caecilian 5, 12, 14
Cane Toad 3, 5, 9, 13, 21, 63, 68, 69, 74
Carpenter Frog 43
Cave-dwelling frog 17
Collared Frog 37.
    See also Rough Frog, Little Frog, Wailing Frog, Short-footed Frog, Daly Waters Frog, Hidden-ear Frog Desert.
    See Knife-footed Frog Grassland.
    See Knife-footed Frog
Cophixalus 66–67
    aenigma 66
    concinnus 66
    monticola 66
    ornatus 13, 66
    saxatilis 10, 66
    zweifeli 66
Corroboree Frog 62–63
    Northern 62, 63
    Southern 62, 63, 72
Creek Frog. See Mistfrog, Common
Crinia 58–60
    bilingua 60
    deserticola 60
    insignifera 59
    nimbus 59
    parinsignifera 59
    remota 60
    riparia 59
    signifera 58
    tasmaniensis 59
    tinnula 11, 59
Crucifix Toad 49
Cyclorana 36–37
    alboguttata 34
    australis 35
    brevipes 37
    cryptotis 37
    cultripes 37
    longipes 37
    maculosa 37
    maini 37
    manya 37
    novaehollandiae 35
    platycephala 36
    vagita 37
    verrucosa 37

D
Dahl's Aquatic Frog 5, 32
Daly Waters Frog 37
Day-frog 50–51
    Eungella 51
    Sharp-snouted 50, 51
        tadpole 50
    Southern 50, 51, 72

E
Elegant Frog 66, 67
Elginerpeton pancheni 14

F
Flat-headed Frog 43
Fletcher's Frog 2, 15, 39
Floodplain Frog. See Bumpy Rocket Frog
Freycinet's Frog 11, 31
Froglet 58–61
    Beeping 59, 60
    Bilingual 60
    Common Eastern 58
    Desert 60
    Haswell's 61
    Moss 59
    Northern 60
    Sign-bearing 59
    Streambank 59
    Tasmanian 59
    Wallum 11, 59
Fry's Frog 67

G
Gastric-brooding Frog 7, 53
    Northern 53
    Southern 53, 72
    tadpoles 7
Geocrinia 61
    laevis 61
    leai 61
    victoriana 61
Giant Frog. See Northern Snapping Frog
Glandular Frog 25
Green-eyed Frog 22
    tadpoles 22
Green-thighed Frog 31, 72
Greenstripe Frog.
    See Burrowing-frog, Striped
Growling Green-eyed Frog 22
Gungan 56–57
    Chubby. See Toadlet, Wrinkled

H
Heleioporus 47
    albopunctatus 47
    australiacus 47
    barycragus 47
    eyrei 47
    inornatus 47
    psammophilus 47
Hidden-ear Frog 36, 37
Holy Cross Frog.
    See Crucifix Toad
Hylidae (family) 16–37

J
Javelin Frog 27

K
Knife-footed Frog 37
Koolasuchus cleelandi 14, 15
Kunapalari Frog 9, 48

L
Labyrinthodonts 14, 79
Lace-lids 28
    Australian 28, 29
Lea's Frog 61
Lechriodus fletcheri 15, 39
Lesueur's Frog 29
Liem's Frog. See Eungella Tinkerfrog
Limnodynastes 42–45
    convexiusculus 9, 43
    depressus 43
    dorsalis 44
    dumerilii 45
    fletcheri 42
    interioris 45
    lignarius 43
    peronii 7, 42
    salmini 43
    tasmaniensis 15, 42
    terraereginae 13, 44
Limnodynastidae (family) 38–48
Litoria 16–37
    adelaidensis 27
    andiirrmalin 28
    aurea 33
    bicolor 27
    brevipalmata 31
    burrowsae 25
    caerulea 13, 16
    castanea 33
    cavernicola 17
    chloris 6, 19
    citropa 25
    cooloolensis 27
    cyclorhyncha 33
    dahlii 5, 32
    daviesae 25
    dentata 26
    electrica 26
    eucnemis 22
    ewingii 23
    freycineti 11, 31
    genimaculata 5, 22
    gilleni 17
    gracilenta 4, 5, 9, 18
    inermis 30
    infrafrenata 13, 17
    jervisiensis 23
    jungguy 29
    latopalmata 30
    lesueuri 29
    littlejohni 23
    longirostris 27
    lorica 28
    lutea 22
    meiriana 29
    microbelos 27
    moorei 33
    myola 22
    nannotis 12, 28
    nasuta 31
    nigrofrenata 31
    nyakalensis 28
    olongburensis 10, 27
    pallida 31
    paraewingi 23
    pearsoniana 24
    peronii 20
    personata 7, 29
    phyllochroa 24
    piperata 25
    raniformis 33
    revelata 23
    rheocola 28
    rothii 5, 9, 21
    rubella 6, 26
    spenceri 29
    splendida 17
    subglandulosa 25
    thesaurensis 22
    tornieri 30
    tyleri 21
    verreauxii 23, 24
    verreauxii alpina 24
    verreauxii verreauxii 24
    wilcoxii 11, 29
    wotjulumensis 6
    xanthomera 19
Little Frog 37
Long-footed Frog 37
Long-snouted Frog 27, 73
Long-thumbed Frog.
    See Barking Frog
Loveridge's Frog 40, 41

M
Main's Frog 37
Marsh-frog 42–43. See also Salmon-striped Frog, Carpenter Frog, Flat-headed Frog, Barking Frog
    Marbled 9, 43
    Spotted 15, 42
    Striped 7, 42, 43, 71
        tadpoles 7
    Western 47
Marsupial Frog 52
Masked Frog 7, 29
    tadpole 7
Meeowing Frog.
    See Sudell's Frog
Metacrinia nichollsi 63
Microhylidae (family) 66–67
Microhylids 66–67
Mistfrogs 28–29
    Common 28, 72
    Mountain 28
Mixophyes 54–55
    balbus 54
    carbinensis 55
    coggeri 55
    fasciolatus 54
    fleayi 10, 55
    hihihorlo 54
    iteratus 13, 55
    schevilli 55
Moaning Frog 47
Motorbike Frogs 33
Mountain Frog 40–41. See also Loveridge's Frog, Baw Baw Frog, Sphagnum Frog
    Masked. See Loveridge's Frog
    Red and Yellow 41
Mount Glorious Torrent Frog.
    See Southern Day Frog
Myobatrachidae (family) 50–64
Myobatrachus gouldii 64

N
Neobatrachus 48
    aquilonius 48
    centralis 48
    kunapalari 9, 48
    pelobatoides 48
    pictus 48
    sudelli 49
    sutor 48
    wilsmorei 48
New Holland Frog.
    See Eastern Snapping Frog
Notaden 49
    bennettii 49
    melanoscaphus 49
    nichollsi 9, 11, 49
    weigeli 49
Nursery-frog 66
    Mountain-top 66
    Ornate 13, 66
    Tapping 66
Nyakala Frog.
    See Mistfrog, Mountain
Nyctimystes dayi 28

O
Opisthodon 46–47
    ornatus 46
    spenceri 11, 46, 47

P
Pale Frog 31
Paracrinia haswelli 61
Parotosuchus gungunj 14
Peppered Frog 25
Peter's Frog. See Bumpy Rocket Frog
Philora 40–41
    frosti 40
    loveridgei 41
    pughi 40
    richmondensis 41
    sphagnicolus 41
Plains Frog 47
Platypus frogs 7, 53
    tadpoles 7
Pleione's Torrent Frog 51
Pouched Frog 10, 52
Prosalirus bitis 15
Pseudophryne 62–63
    australis 10, 63
    corroboree 62
    covacevichae 63
    major 63
    pengilleyi 62